For the Love of
NETWORKING

How to put successful networking at the heart of your business and life

JOHN HARVEY
Founder of The Samphire Club

For the Love of Networking
ISBN 978-1-912300-70-9
eISBN 978-1-912300-71-6

Published in 2022 by Right Book Press
Printed in the UK

A CIP record of this book is available from the British Library.

Contents

Acknowledgements

The idea for this book originated over a coffee and a chat in Plymouth with Julian Summerhays. He was kind enough to introduce me to Sonja Nisson and Sharon Tanton in Bristol, who in turn introduced me to Sue Richardson. I would also like to thank...

Eva Seymour at Well Put Words: the keeper of my tone of voice and whose expertise and friendship is a huge part of the success of The Samphire Club.

Andrew Tapson: my finance director, who keeps me in check and provides invaluable advice and friendship.

Garry Langan for taking me under his wing towards the end of year one and providing much-needed support and advice.

Joanne Manville: my long-suffering VA who ensures that everything runs smoothly. I like to think I'm her high-maintenance client!

Lucy Thomas and Sam Linggard: my accountants who provide professional advice and support, and are a joy to work with.

Hazel Parsons and Jenny Granlund. For organising my events in the early years and providing their support and expertise.

Mark Smith, who encouraged me in my early days of networking and who has kindly written the foreword for this book.

Robert Camp and Mandy Reynolds: for their support and advice from the start and their ongoing help and encouragement.

Mark Godfrey: whose ongoing support and friendship has taught me so much about the hospitality approach to customer experience.

Jason Parry: another hospitality mentor whose advice and support has been much appreciated.

The senior team at the Pig Hotels: who have made me feel part of the family and who are major supporters of the club.

Ben Young: another hospitality mentor who has been a supporter from the beginning and who continues to lend advice and support.

Verity Slater: who provided an invaluable piece of legal advice in the early days and saved me from a potentially toxic situation.

Agne Seikyte and Fiona Darde: they allowed me to make the Hotel Du Vin in Exeter my home from home.

Nicole Yearshon: for her advice, support and friendship.

Robin Barker: for his advice and support and welcome into his world of hospitality.

James Nettledon and Laura Cameron: for their ongoing support and encouragement.

Clive Kessell: for his boundless enthusiasm and positive vibes!

Chris Mugford: for his encouragement and advice at the start and the beautiful film he created.

Foreword

I first met John Harvey a little over a decade ago, when I came to work for an urban regeneration company in Cornwall. When you arrive in a new role, existing colleagues are always quick to suggest people to meet, those who add value to your work and are active in the business community. John was cited as one of those people.

I remember entering a room full of people: John was quick to come over and provide a warm welcome, rapidly establish rapport and start introducing me to people he thought would have attributes that would be useful in my work. I knew then that he was a natural at connecting people, and our friendship has endured from that moment. Why? You'll find the answer to that in this book. John and I have collaborated on and off for over a decade, using our connection to build opportunities for each other and the diverse networks we have cultivated.

This is because, as you will read, John's approach to networking stems from a basic belief that humans all do best when they connect on a personal level, sharing the joy of finding out more about each other, defining and supporting shared goals. This book, then, focuses on the long-term benefit of a mutual approach, and sets out simple but key attributes for building successful business relationships. The principles he establishes are straightforward but highly effective, and will become a powerful part of your toolkit.

Reading though this book, I smile at the honesty of the thoughts he has beautifully expressed, and just how they reflect John's own joys gained from cultivating a broad and responsive network. Not everyone will perhaps initially believe that the approaches he describes can be so effective, but studied and executed in the way he expresses, John's work will help you build connections in business that will last throughout your lifetime, and make your work truly fulfilling. I hope reading this book also brings you joy, and that you pass on the principles you will learn at every opportunity.

Mark Smith
Executive Director of Business & Regional Engagement
Aston University

Introduction

Networking is a word that is widely used: it means different things to different people. For some people such as myself, it is a way of life – and about as much fun you can have with your clothes on! Yet for many people it has negative connotations and not something with which that they feel comfortable. It can conjure up images of men in suits at a breakfast or lunch meeting, and being forced to endure yet another elevator pitch while juggling a cup of tea and a business card!

Most organisations view networking as an important business activity without fully understanding what it is, or how to do it effectively. Employees are often expected to network without being given the necessary training or tools to perform effectively. Whichever camp you're in, networking is a permanent fixture on the business landscape – and ironically, most of us network every day without realising it!

I first became aware of networking as a thing when I moved back to Cornwall after many years in London. Ironically back then we networked all the time, but it was referred to as 'schmoozing'! I had one job that required me to attend the Cannes Film Festival and the American Film Market – networking at the glamorous end of the scale. During my London years I was a member of a leading private members' club, which instilled in me the power of community and the primeval need of human beings to belong to a tribe.

Fast forward to Cornwall, where I was taken to a weekly breakfast meeting in Falmouth which I subsequently attended on behalf of the company I was working for (confession: in those early days I viewed it as an opportunity to get out of the office and enjoy a free breakfast!). My journey led me to the Cornwall Chamber of Commerce, and I soon became immersed in the local business community. It was here that my love affair with the world of networking began.

I attended as many events as I could, devoured books on the subject and went to hear experts speak on the topic. I was like a sponge absorbing knowledge as my fascination took hold. In a twist of fate, my job role changed and I ended up having to network full-time. As a result I learned on the job, attended every networking event possible and soon extended my reach into Devon and latterly, Somerset and Bristol. As my network grew, I was fortunate to meet many people who were kind enough to share their knowledge and wisdom and guide me on my journey. Speaking opportunities arose as my reputation grew, as did my desire to share my increasing knowledge and connections.

Again, fate intervened and my dream job came to an end. I remember an evening of drinks at the Greenbank Hotel in Falmouth, when some bright spark suggested I monetise my networking expertise. Given that I never take an introducer's fee or a cut of any subsequent business that results, I struggled to see how this would work.

The conversation switched to the location of the best networking opportunities within Cornwall. Although I was heavily involved with the Cornwall Chamber, experience had taught me that Chambers of Commerce generally have very little understanding of networking, and are not able to provide valuable networking opportunities for the vast majority of their members.

To me, the best networking opportunities occur at events that are private, by invitation and off-diary – if you're not in the room, you're unlikely to know they take place. By this time, I had hosted such an event in a private dining room in Newquay, and knew how valuable this type of networking could be.

Starting a business and working for myself had never been on my radar, but now the opportunity to do so was staring me in the face. After a great deal of soul-searching and many conversations with people in my network, I decided to take the plunge. I had little expectation of success, and fully expected to be back in a paid role within a year or two. My business plan was simply to survive year one without running out of money. I was able to draw down some pension, which allowed me to fund the business initially, and part of me wanted to experience something new.

I had a clear vision of what The Samphire Club could be, but no idea how to make that a reality. The good news was that I had a robust network, which allowed me access to a reservoir of knowledge, expertise and support. Even so, I made numerous mistakes and ended up experiencing serious burnout. At this point my network came to my aid, and various people emerged to offer help and guidance. Six years later, the club has evolved into a community of like-minded organisations and individuals who buy into the ethos of collaboration, knowledge-sharing, expertise and mutual support.

Originally, I was not convinced the world needed another book on networking, but over time my desire to share my knowledge and experiences grew. Networking in its purest form is the sharing of knowledge, expertise, and contacts without expectation of anything in return. It's about developing strong relationships that lead to opportunities and often friendships.

This book contains everything that I hold dear; it's based on my understanding and experience of all things networking. Networking is the art of being true to your own values, beliefs and character, while building and nurturing reciprocal relationships that help individuals or the group as a whole to achieve their goals.

Having networked full-time for more than a decade and established a business on the back of it, I know better than most the power and value of networking. It has transformed my life beyond all recognition. These days my time is spent on building the Samphire community and supporting the membership in any way I can. I work with a number of organisations, normally centred on networking and business development along with customer experience. I am constantly looking to improve the membership experience and ensure it's both fun and rewarding.

The main purpose of this guide is to demystify the world of networking, and to show what a fun, valuable and rewarding activity it can be. It is designed to be a source of reference for beginners and experts alike.

The recent global pandemic has shone a spotlight on the power of networks and connectivity. With people stuck at home, the need for human connection has been greater than ever – and the value of a robust network even more apparent. Online networking via platforms such as Zoom and Microsoft Teams is here to stay, as is hybrid working – and your approach to networking needs to reflect this.

Who is this guide for?

It's for:

→ anyone embarking on their journey into the world of networking

→ individuals who attend or have attended a networking event, and either not enjoyed the experience or come away unsure if it's the best use of their time

→ the corporate world sending staff to events who want to see a better return on time and resources – particularly sales management and finance directors

→ students entering the workplace – networking is an essential life skill that employers value highly

→ expert networkers who already know their stuff – please comment and add to the debate!

How to use this guide

It can be read from start to finish like any other book, or dipped into whenever the mood takes you. It is also there to be referred to when you are planning to attend an event, to help with preparation and research. It's a companion to take with you to an event, to act as a reminder. After the event, it can be your first port of call when you follow up, to gain maximum value from your attendance.

If you like it, please feel free to recommend it to your own network.

Why another book on networking?

As I'm sure you are aware, there is a plethora of books on the subject – and I have read most of them! Among my favourites are: *The Financial Times Guide to Business*

Networking (2011) by Heather Townsend, and *Never Eat Alone* (2014) by Keith Ferrazzi (see Bibliography and further reading at the end of this book). There is a danger that another general book on the subject could be misconstrued as an indulgence – or worse still, an ego trip. I wanted to find a way to share my knowledge and experience with a wider audience, but at the same time to concentrate on the specific area of events within the wider subject.

I know that attending events works, and am passionate about helping people and organisations both understand the subtleties involved, and use the methods and skills I have learned throughout my career to hugely positive effect.

Let me introduce you to my world, where the emphasis is on being nice and fun is normal. Networking has the power to change your life, as it has mine!

1 What is networking?

For many people, networking is seen as a business activity that is encouraged by their employer or they need to do to grow their business. It is often viewed as necessary, but not always enjoyable.

For me, it's a way of life and a mindset – it has fundamentally changed my life and allowed me to establish a business based on people and hospitality. I have an ongoing love affair with networking and all that comes with it; every day is an adventure that involves spending time with people and organisations, and looking for ways to help them. I like to say that I sprinkle fairy dust, leaving them feeling better as a result!

There are many different definitions of networking. Some of my favourites are as follows:

Carole Stone:

Networking is making the most of the people you meet to your mutual benefit. (Stone 2004, in D'Souza 2008).

Steven D'Souza:

Networking is the art of being true to your own values, beliefs, and character while building and nurturing reciprocal relationships that help individuals in the group as a whole to achieve their goals. (D'Souza 2008)

Andy Lopata:

> Networking isn't about groups and organisations, they merely facilitate it. Networking is, and should be about people and should occur naturally. (Lopata 2011)

Jan Vermeiren:

> In a sales process the goal of the interaction between two people is the sale of a product or service. When networking this sale could be the consequence of a contact that is built with respect and care. So it is clear that the sale is not the goal of networking but a welcome and in many cases logical consequence. (Vermeiren 2007)

My definition:

> Networking is any activity that increases the value of your network and/or the value you contribute to it. It is about building and nurturing a community built on reciprocal relationships – and making people smile.

Because, as Andy Lopata points out, networking is about people, so the following factors come into play: perception, values, feelings and behaviour. These are not fixed, and all change over time. They are fluid and unpredictable, which makes them extremely difficult to measure (a major reason why, for example, finance directors find networking so difficult).

Something all these definitions have in common is the importance of relationship-building. This is at the heart of what networking is about. It needs to be embraced with a positive mindset: your first instinct must be to seek to help, to give rather than take, and to receive any help with humility and gratitude.

What networking is not

A lot of people mistakenly think that networking is the start of the sales process. The danger of this is damaging their credibility and risking becoming unpopular.

Networking is not about sales or selling, and pitching should be avoided. There are organisations and groups that operate on this principle: they suit some people but can put others off networking, especially if it's their first experience. To avoid any misunderstandings, these meetings would be better described as sales groups. In fact, networking is much more subtle, and the benefits accrue over time as you build social capital.

A consequence of using networking mainly as a sales tool is that many people and organisations approach networking with an expectation of immediate return on investment, which inevitably leads to disappointment. A better approach is to look for return on engagement or return on relationships, as advocated by Ted Rubin in his excellent book *Return on Relationships* (2014).

Making connections

A *network* is an entity that consists of a number of things that are connected (for example, in the way that we talk about a rail network or a computer network).

The 'net' in 'network'

Your network is your safety net: it can protect you from everything life might throw at you, and should include everyone you might need at some point. Obvious examples are friends, but also a plumber, electrician and builder.

Problem-solving

When I'm faced with any issue, my first instinct is to turn to my network, and my trust in it is absolute.

A recent example: my cottage has a major damp problem, which was discovered by my decorator. After obtaining quotes and suggestions from several builders, I was a little overwhelmed.

At this point I turned to my network and realised that I have a firm of surveyors within it who were more than happy to help. They prevented me from wasting time and money on bad advice.

Even if you don't have a direct connection, somebody in your network will know someone who has the solution.

To return to the idea of a net: to build a network, it's essential to cast far and wide. Seek out new networking opportunities, and be prepared to travel. A common mistake is that people fall into a comfortable routine, networking in the same groups with the same people without ever feeling the need to change.

I too fell into this trap when I first started networking.

Starting out

I started my networking journey at the Falmouth Business Club, and had no clue what I was doing. It quickly became a fun group of people that I enjoyed spending time with, but after a while it became dreadfully stale and a bit like *Groundhog Day*. I always sat at the same end of the table with the same people (a bit like the back seat of the bus on school trips).

What made me move was the appearance at the other end of the table of a business development executive of a company I wanted as a client. This was one of the first significant steps in my journey: we became networking buddies and worked the Cornwall circuit together – and yes, her employer did become a client.

She is now the head of business development at a major law firm, and is still one of my most valued contacts.

The lesson here is that the more diverse reciprocal relationships you have, the more you will benefit from potential options and opportunities.

The 'work' in 'network'

It isn't possible to build a powerful network without a lot of hard work – remember, it's a lifetime's work, not a sprint. I refer to the initial phase as the 'grunt work': you don't get good at something without practice. In the early stages it can feel like pushing a boulder up a hill, and so dispiriting. Fear of rejection and looking foolish are normal, and very real.

I have yet to discover a shortcut, and after ten years of networking full-time, I am still happy to put in the work. (Equally, I'm single without children, which gives me a certain advantage.) The good news is that it does become easier and, as you get more accomplished, it becomes a fun, rewarding activity that will provide you with hours of entertainment as well as many rewards.

Six Degrees of Separation

In 1967, Stanley Milgram, a professor at Yale University, developed the theory known as 'Six Degrees of Separation' – now so widely recognised that books have been written, films produced and even a game invented around the idea ('Six Degrees of Kevin Bacon'). The theory states that we are only six steps away from anyone in the world (Milgram 1967).

In his experiment, Milgram mailed a name and address to 160 people who lived in Omaha, Nebraska. In every package the name was the same: a stockbroker who lived in Sharon, Massachusetts and worked in Boston. Each recipient was asked to write their name on the package and post it to someone they knew on a first-name basis, whom they thought most likely to know the broker. That person would then write their own name on the package and send it on a step closer in turn, until the package finally arrived at the stockbroker's house.

Once all the packages had been received by the broker, Milgram was able to track back through the steps each package had taken on its journey. He found that most of the packages had taken five or six steps to reach their destination. Interestingly, a number of the packages had been routed through the same small number of people (I refer to these as 'super connectors' – see Ferrazzi 2014).

In 2001 Duncan Watts, a professor at Columbia University, continued his own earlier research into the phenomenon by recreating Milgram's experiment on the Internet. Watts used an email message as the 'package' that needed to be delivered. Surprisingly, after reviewing the data collected by 48,000 senders and 19 targets (in 157 countries), Watts found that the average number of intermediaries was, indeed, six (Watts 2004).

This is important with regard to networking, as it shows how possible it is to connect to people in our world – particularly someone who is in business in the same region or country as us. The good news is that we are unlikely to need the full six steps (in Cornwall, we say it's three – with a cousin thrown in somewhere!).

When you appreciate this, the potential of networking becomes vast.

Looking after your network

An analogy I like to use here is treating your network as you would an allotment: give it attention on a daily basis. I understand that if I look after it, it will in turn look after me. In the short term, it will provide produce to sustain me in the form of contacts and knowledge, but over a lifetime it will provide a harvest. I aim to plant new seeds daily in the form of new connections, and water my network daily by reaching out to connections and keeping in contact with them. I also weed it by removing contacts that prove to be unhealthy.

I would suggest you spend some time daily attending to your network if you wish to reap the rewards it can provide. These include endless opportunities, both business and personal. It is potentially the most valuable asset you have, so treat it with the respect it deserves. It is your bank of social capital.

As Heather Townsend describes it:

> Social capital is the imaginary bank account that you build up by being helpful to people. It can be measured by the breadth and the depth of your network, the strength of your relationships within in it, and the goodwill and level of influence you have within your network. (Townsend 2011)

Steven D'Souza:

> Social capital is the concept that value can be created from the structure, size and diversity of your networks, whether personal or professional. (D'Souza 2008)

(To explore this subject in more depth, see *Achieving Success Through Social Capital* by Wayne Baker – see Bibliography and further reading at the end of this book.)

The extent of your personal reach and level of influence within your network are key factors in generating the opportunities you want and need. Social capital has to be earned and accumulated, but it also can be spent. The more goodwill and influence you gain within your network, the greater the amount of social capital you are accumulating. Your level of social capital is enhanced by who you know and are seen with: if you spend time with people with a greater level of prestige, credibility or status, some of that automatically rubs off on you.

Success isn't solely down to your individual efforts and abilities; it is also social and depends on the quality of your network.

Networking is also a state of mind rather than just an activity you indulge in: an attitude that manifests itself in willingness to help people and seek out win–win outcomes. Great networkers subscribe to the principle of 'givers' gain', meaning that you have to give first in order to receive. Too many people I meet on my travels get this the wrong way around.

Ways to network

There are two major ways to network: in-person and online. Face-to-face allows you to look into people's eyes and gain an impression that you cannot replicate online. However, social media affords you a huge reach, allowing you to connect with people and organisations that you cannot do conventionally. The vast majority of people and organisations have an online presence and use social media (for more on this, see Chapter 5).

Is one more important than the other? No. It's essential to do both – if you want to build your network.

In conclusion, networking is something we all do in our

daily lives without being conscious of it. Examples include belonging to a sports club, meeting a friend for a catch-up, looking at social media, the school run and other school activities, funerals, weddings, talking to people in queues, doing team activities at work. I don't consciously decide to network anymore; it's what defines my life.

A powerful network is the single most valuable asset you can own, and as mentioned previously, will sustain you for life if looked after properly. Networking takes time and should be viewed as a long-term investment. Although it is not about sales and selling, it should be a major part of your business development effort, whether you are an individual or an organisation. The reason that it isn't is normally due to a fundamental lack of understanding (especially within the finance community) and an absence of strategy.

Networking can be learned, and everybody can become proficient with training and practice.

Key takeaways

➡ Networking is about building and maintaining relationships.
➡ Your network is the most valuable thing you have, and will sustain you for life – tend to it daily.
➡ Networking is not about selling!

Networking tip

Networking is more than an activity. It has to come from a good place, with good intentions.

2 Why network?

People choose to network for a variety of reasons. It's a great way to meet people who can be customers, investors, partners or friends. It can provide you with the information you need to make decisions, and teach you things you didn't know before. It's a way of connecting with valuable expertise and resources.

Networking can help you land your dream job, assist with promotion and enhance your career. Any issue that benefits from others' support is far easier to deal with if you have a robust network on which to rely. A strong network allows you to make your mark on the world, so it's beholden on you to use your network to do good.

This chapter focuses on how networking can help with:

➡ business development – generating new opportunities, such as new clients or a new job
➡ enhancing your career – raising your profile, which helps with career development
➡ knowledge-seeking and sharing
➡ building a network that supports you for life.

– whichever applies to you, networking is the most powerful way to achieve all of these aims.

Effective networking enables you to become known as an expert in your field – a guru, which in turn raises your profile and leads people and opportunities to you. Word-of-mouth marketing is extremely successful – and it's free! The power of a personal recommendation can't be underestimated, especially in the case of high-value purchases where the buyer is looking to mitigate the risk involved. (Ask yourself: how did you find your plumber or builder?)

Networking has been around since trade began, and Chambers of Commerce have been in existence since the 1700s. Today, it is more important than ever, as the world has changed enormously with the development of the Internet. The new knowledge-based, global economy has given people far more choice, and they are far better informed. Your customers – and competitors – can be anywhere in the world. Standing still isn't an option: adapt or die! People's attention span has shrunk: they're looking for instant gratification, and instinctively use their networks to find what they are looking for. With the rise of online networking via social media, it is now possible to build a large and engaged network.

As Dan Schawbel said, back in 2009:

> You are now competing with everyone on a global scale. There is no job security at all, and now it is all about being found instead of submitting your résumé. Networking is the way to be found, and how the smart people get jobs and opportunities now. That is the big difference from even five years ago. (Schawbel 2009)

Business development

Traditionally, business development is based on sales and marketing, with a huge emphasis on new business and client acquisition. When I started my career in sales many years ago, my targets and key performance indicators were all based on new business. My entire focus was on hitting my numbers, which were discussed at a quarterly review meeting with the senior bods from head office. Client service and experience were not my concern – a fundamental weakness of such an antiquated system!

I have been on more sales training courses than I care to remember, and have been taught how to manage a pipeline, overcome objections and close sales. I have been taught that people buy people – which isn't strictly accurate. People buy from people *that they like*, and it is that bit on the end that is relevant to the importance of networking (as will be explained in Chapter 4).

This approach to business development is incredibly time-consuming and expensive. It's also a very crude system based on tradition. The fundamental flaw is that in general, people do not like being sold to – the payment protection insurance (PPI) scandal (in which insurance was mis-sold by banks and financial companies between the 1970s and 2000s), along with a breakdown in trust in experts, haven't helped. People are far better informed, have far more choice and prefer to buy themselves. (When did you last use a travel agent to arrange a holiday?)

Likeability

Networking is the activity that enables you to demonstrate your expertise, standing and, most importantly, likeability. You can demonstrate likeability to your community (both on and offline), which in turn strengthens your relationships to the point that people or organisations trust you and want to buy from you. All of this takes a significant investment of time and commitment. (Equally there are some people who, however good your offering and intentions, will never buy from you because they just don't like you. So get over it and move on!)

Influencers

Another way in which networking can help with business development is to build a group of influencers or brand ambassadors within your network. These are often professional services such as bankers, accountants and lawyers who have clients of their own and influence. It is a system which they both understand and use, and is powerful. A personal recommendation from a lawyer or accountant tends to be taken seriously.

> ## My personal experience
> In a previous role I was required to build relationships with companies who were involved with import/export. It occurred to me that the professional services companies would know these companies.
>
> The UK & Trade and Investment advisors had to generate their own leads, and it occurred to us that the people who had this information were the banks, accountants and law firms!
>
> For networking to be effective and produce meaningful results, it has to be strategic and an integral part of your marketing plan (and for the more enlightened, the major thrust of your business development).

Career enhancement

As Dan Schawbel (2009) says, job security is a thing of the past. Now, people will have a number of different jobs in their working life. We have seen the rise of the 'mixed portfolio' option, where people have several separate roles simultaneously. The chances are you will be made redundant at least once in your working life; it's how you deal with it that defines your future prospects. For millennials and Generation Z, the competition for top jobs is intense.

People who are well networked are more than twice as likely to be headhunted. They are known within their field and may be regarded as experts. They are easy to find (on LinkedIn, for example) and likely to have a strong network which they know how to leverage.

Understanding the recruitment process

It is important to understand the situation of filling a post from the company's perspective. When you lose an employee you suddenly have a gap, and that person's work has to be absorbed by your existing staff until a replacement can be found. This immediately puts a strain on your existing resources, and has a cost in terms of time and money.

How to fill the position? Traditionally, you placed an advertisement in a newspaper or the relevant trade journal and invited candidates to submit their CVs. You then compiled an applicant shortlist to invite for interview. This often led to a second round of interviews before the position was filled – a slow and expensive process.

The recruitment process has changed enormously, and is now a completely different beast. Jobs still do get advertised in newspapers and magazines, but increasingly companies turn to recruitment agencies or headhunters – which is especially true for more senior positions. It is a good example of outsourcing function-as-efficiency: let somebody else do the search, and draw up a list of candidates. However, there is a cost to this in terms of agency fees, and it can still be a slow process.

The more aware companies first look to their own network (both internal and external), and those of their employees. They recognise that not only is it important to find somebody capable of fulfilling the role, but also far more important that they fit the culture of the organisation or the specific team if it is that type of role. Companies are looking increasingly for people with the right attitude and attributes, as they can train them for the role. Some more enlightened companies recruit talent and then create a role to suit the candidate.

As a result of this, a lot of jobs are never advertised – in the same way that a lot of top-level properties are sold without ever coming on to the market. We are back to the power of word-of-mouth. Remember, people employ people they like!

Leveraging your network for jobsearch

It is important to use your network and networking activity (both online and face-to-face) to your advantage. As mentioned previously, having a presence and being regarded as an expert in your field means you're far more likely to be found. Publish articles and share material, speak at events and build a personal brand (more of that in Chapter 4).

Draw up a list of companies that you would love to work for, then make a plan to get on their radar. The first step is to engage with them on social media. Twitter allows for an informality that LinkedIn doesn't, and can be a great way to grab attention.

Serendipity at work

I was having lunch with a hotel owner in Cornwall in my first year of Samphire, and her PR company who were based in London came up in conversation. Serendipitously, the managing director of that company suddenly followed me on Twitter, and I received an alert.

I immediately thanked her for the follow, mentioned that I was having lunch with one of her clients, and were her ears burning? She then asked what The Samphire Club was. I suggested she email me, and I would tell her. As a result of this engagement, I met with her on my next trip to London and the company subsequently became a member of the club.

Equally important is to go to events where your chosen companies will be in attendance, so that you bump into them. Later in the guide I will explain how you go about this, but the aim is to start a relationship with them and get on their radar. It's perfectly acceptable to tell them that you would love to work for them at some point: they are likely to remember this, so if a position does come up, you are somebody they can approach direct.

Aim to build relationships with as many people in the company as possible and at different levels. Trust me, they will research you and keep you in mind, provided you make the right impression.

Gaining knowledge

I refer to gaining knowledge as a 'learning safari': you are never too old to learn, and knowledge is a powerful thing. A lot of networking events feature a speaker; there are numerous other opportunities out there. Conferences are a great investment (Chapter 7 will explain how to maximise the benefits of attending such an event).

Other good examples are TED events, or any thought leadership events such as Like Minds in Exeter.

Aim to read articles online as part of your networking strategy. If you are well-read on a subject, it helps create a memorable impression when you meet somebody and engage in conversation with them.

Knowledge-sharing

Sharing your knowledge helps in a number of ways. As mentioned previously, it raises your profile and establishes you as a perceived expert in your field. It helps you gain a following and build a community, which in turn helps you to be found and increases your chances of being headhunted.

Lastly, this is one of the fundamental pillars of networking: sharing your knowledge and contacts without any expectation of something in return.

Building a network that looks after you for life

This is the idea of tending your allotment (as discussed in Chapter 1). A powerful network helps you build a profitable, sustainable business, and enables you to find the right people or others to find you. It also helps in your private life: you might find your partner from within your network! As mentioned previously, I urge you to embrace this because it will enrich your life in so many different ways and enable you to handle whatever life throws at you.

In conclusion, there are many reasons to network and at some point they will all apply to you – so jump on board and get started.

Key takeaways

➡ Networking is vital for business development, career enhancement and recruitment.

➡ Networking helps you to build and share your knowledge.

Networking tip

Whatever reason you choose to network (business development, career enhancement), enjoyment and success are more likely if you employ strategy.

3 Where and when to network

This chapter discusses where to network and the frequency of your activity, as this will be an integral part of your networking strategy.

As highlighted previously, the two basic forms of networking are in-person and virtual: it is important to do both. We will look at both business and social networking because both provide huge opportunities to develop your network.

Your frequency of networking activity will depend on your workload, but it should be a basic component of both your business development effort and career enhancement. Time of day will be a factor, as will the day of the week – especially if you are planning your own events.

Opportunities for networking in person

To the majority of people I meet on my travels, networking is seen as a business activity that involves attending organised events. For many it is something to be endured because they have been told to attend or feel they ought to do so. There is a wide range of options available to you.

Chambers of Commerce

Chambers of Commerce play a prominent role in the business community. They tend to be male-dominated and a bit formal, but are a good way to meet a cross-section of the business community.

Because Chambers of Commerce are obligated to offer a showcase to their members, their event format often lacks effectiveness, as the time available to talk is interrupted by presentations by members which are effectively glorified sales pitches. Their weakness is that there is a danger that they become self-serving, and can be ego-driven. In my experience, business owners tend to avoid them, as they are time-poor and prefer not to be pitched to by lawyers and accountants!

My advice would be to go as a guest before committing to membership, and certainly review your membership annually.

The other leading business groups include the Confederation of British Industry (CBI), Institute of Directors (IoD) and Federation of Small Businesses (FSB).

Confederation of British Industry

The CBI is a not-for-profit membership organisation founded in 1965. It represents businesses and provides a voice for firms to policymakers. Membership is expensive and aimed towards companies. Its events are an opportunity to meet senior businesspeople, but tend to be a little dry.

Institute of Directors

The IoD is an organisation for company directors, senior business leaders and entrepreneurs. It was founded in 1903 and incorporated by Royal Charter in 1906. As per its mission statement, it stands for free enterprise, entrepreneurialism, wealth creation and good corporate governance. It represents the views of business and IoD members in the media and with government. One of the key benefits of membership is access to its headquarters in London's Pall Mall and other co-working spaces around the UK (but this is less important with the emergence of private members' clubs).

Federation of Small Businesses

The FSB represents smaller businesses and offers its members a wide range of business services including advice, financial expertise, support and a powerful voice heard in government.

All of these organisations have a mission to lobby government and are expensive, as they have staff and offices to maintain. They all offer networking opportunities, and I have found them to be very good. However, they are a little 'pale, male and stale': the world of work has changed enormously, and they need to adapt to remain relevant. For a business contemplating membership, do detailed research and insist on attendance as a guest before committing.

Breakfast clubs

There are also smaller, less formal groups such as breakfast clubs: for example, BNI (Business Network International), where the emphasis is much more on generating sales and return on investment (ROI). These work for a lot of individuals (tradespeople and sole traders) but can lack senior figures from larger organisations.

Sector-specific groups

Specific groups (e.g. property, construction, food and drink, manufacturing and hospitality) offer excellent opportunities if you want to become known in your sector, or you wish to work with a particular sector. (In the next chapter we will look at sector-driven networking, which should be an integral part of your strategy.)

Events and conferencing

Many professional service companies host their own events, and attendance is either via invitation or a mailing list. The quality of the audience tends to be high as a result. Award ceremonies and charity events provide excellent networking opportunities and allow you to build credibility via familiarity.

Conferences and events such as TED talks are another source of opportunity to get in front of senior businesspeople. Lastly, consider hosting your own events, where you can control the variables to achieve the desired outcomes (more on this in Chapter 9).

Networking outside the workplace

All of us network daily without necessarily being conscious of it. Any occasion where we interact or engage with other people is networking – we just don't think of it like that. Sports clubs and gyms are an obvious example (for example, the gig rowing scene in the south-west is a tribe in its own right), as is any activity linked to school. Parents tend to chat to other parents at the school gate and form part of a social group, especially if the children are friends. I often find examples of businesses working together because of this connection.

Another area is religion, where people of faith tend to

have their own network. (This is certainly my experience in Exeter, where there is a group of businesspeople who go to the same church have a strong bond as a result.)

Rotary and Round Table are two historic organisations that provide excellent networking opportunities, along with a charitable function.

Travel offers excellent networking opportunities – be it on the train or at the airport, it's a question of being open to possibilities. I recently recruited a new member to the club after he met my sister on a train!

Although a lot of people do not like work commitments on a weekend, sporting events are always productive and offer a rare opportunity to bump into business owners and senior professionals. (The Exeter Chiefs rugby games provide one of the richest networking opportunities in the south-west.)

Other opportunities for networking

Social media

Because social media involves engagement, it is networking by another name. Like networking in our social lives, most people are blissfully unaware that they network daily via this route!

We will look at the different platforms (LinkedIn, Twitter, Instagram, WhatsApp and Facebook) in more detail in Chapter 5, but one or more of these platforms should be an integral part of your networking activity.

Direct contact

How many of you send handwritten notes to your staff or customers? Try it sometime. Another old-fashioned method is the phone, which is frequently neglected in this modern age. A courtesy call to a client can be an effective way to strengthen an existing relationship.

Email marketing
This is another excellent networking opportunity: any business that doesn't have a mailing list is missing a hugely valuable way of engaging with their community.

Professional forums
These are excellent places to build your network, allowing you to engage with people or organisations that you have identified. The key is to get involved and engage, post a comment and go with the engagement that follows. It's also a great opportunity for you to demonstrate your knowledge and expertise.

Blogs
These are a great way to engage with a wider audience, (I had a blog long before I set up The Samphire Club. It was titled 'Canapés & Conversations: A diary of a Cornish networker'.) If you are invited to guest on other people's blogs, accept – it's another way to get noticed and validate your expertise.

Podcasts
These have exploded in recent years, and are now a powerful way of engaging with a huge audience. As with blogs, they are a great way to demonstrate your expertise and build your tribe. The key thing to note is that you must be prepared to give away your knowledge and expertise for free – which may seem counter-intuitive.

These days it isn't difficult to start: a good smartphone is all you need. Start small, and practise before launching.

It's also good to be invited on to other people's podcasts, as again it validates your expertise and raises your professional standing.

When and how often to network

To make networking work for you, it's important to show up on a consistent basis, as relationships are built over time. How you do this depends on what you want to achieve, and how much time you are prepared to commit. I would urge you to engage in a business-related activity at least once a week as a bare minimum, and engage online daily.

I'm regularly told by people that they don't have time for social media – and often they do have busy schedules. However, everybody can free up five minutes twice a day to engage online. It's not a question of time, but attitude. Networking is still regarded as an extra rather than an integral part of business activity. If you can't commit to a daily routine, it is probably better to avoid it – as dipping in and out creates a bad impression.

For an organisation, networking should be part of your business development effort: it is essential to be active in the community and online. Some companies have a rota to cover more events (spreading their net wide): it makes sense to do this, as different events attract a certain type of audience.

Networking events take place at different times of day, which has a bearing on who can attend (many professionals have to work around school runs), as well as different days of the week.

I would encourage you to build a portfolio of different events and see what works for you. Some people prefer to get it done first thing and enjoy breakfast events, while other people are better after work. For some, family commitments come into play; while for others, Friday evening is not always an optimum time to arrange an event, as it encroaches on the weekend. Lunch can be an excellent time, but it can be difficult for senior business leaders who have full schedules and are usually time-poor.

Coffee, cake and conversations

Something I introduced is what I refer to as 'coffee and cake', which was suggested by my accountant. As a mother of two she had a school run in the morning, which made it extremely difficult to attend breakfast events. As head of the practice she rarely has time to do a lunchtime event, and evenings are taken up with family commitments.

I choose a location (normally a hotel), and base myself there for the morning. The event runs from 9.30 am to 11 am and is open to all, with no requirement to book. There is no agenda or speaker, so people can drop in and leave to suit their schedule. I provide pastries and cake, and people buy themselves tea or coffee. They take pot luck as to who they might meet, but this can be mitigated by discussing the event beforehand via social media. The key point is that I will be there and will know everybody who drops in, enabling me to act as host and make the necessary introductions.

It has proved popular with professionals with families who drop in after the school run, and freelancers (working from home) who want some human interaction. As its main cost is the price of a hot drink, it's also affordable.

Networking is a state of mind as well as an activity. I'm always subconsciously open to networking opportunities, carrying business cards and speaking to people in social situations.

Key takeaways

➡ Incorporate a mix of face-to-face and virtual networking into your strategy.

➡ Remember that networking doesn't just take place in a business environment.

➡ Networking should be a daily activity.

Networking tip

Major sporting events are excellent opportunities to network, and for example, in the south-west we are spoilt with various rugby teams and cricket at Taunton. If you are invited, accept without hesitation. It's also a great way to entertain your clients and prospects.

4 Building a networking strategy

This chapter will look at how to network more effectively and build a network for life (tending your allotment, see Chapter 1). It examines the importance of strategy, and the need to have a networking plan that is measured and reviewed regularly. It also looks at the different tools required (mindset, time management), and how to manage your network.

Strategy is the building block on which your networking activity should be based. Most people are familiar with the concept of a business plan and marketing strategy, but it is rare that I come across organisations or individuals with a networking strategy. A strategy is a plan of action designed to achieve a long-term or overall aim. Strategy originated in the military and has been around longer than business.

Planning your strategy

To plan your strategy, you have to establish your overall aim. Are you networking to achieve business growth, career enhancement, find knowledge and answers or a combination of them all? At different times you will need all of these things, so a starting point is to aim to build a powerful, vibrant network that you can call on, and a bank of social capital.

When thinking about your strategy, you will need to consider the following:

- → Who do I want in my network?
- → How can I consolidate existing customers and clients in my network?
- → Do I want to focus on a particular sector?
- → How wide am I prepared to cast my net?
- → How much am I prepared to spend?
- → What mindset and traits will I need to adopt?
- → What are my goals?
- → How much time am I willing to commit to networking?
- → How can I build my network?
- → How can I strengthen my personal brand?
- → How can I maintain my network?

Define who you want in your network

The majority of organisations and individuals I meet network to find business opportunities, and networking is often an add-on to their sales and marketing effort. Although networking is not about sales and selling, with a careful strategy it can be one of the most effective ways to grow a profitable, sustainable business.

Examine your offer

Start by examining your offer and ask yourself what is it that you are providing: for example, insurance is less about the details of the policy, and everything about the peace of mind provided by it. Then examine why people buy, as most people hate being sold to. I learned this on an export course several years ago: people buy for two fundamental reasons, to gain pleasure or avoid pain. The insurance example falls into the latter category, although there may be some pleasure in the peace of mind afforded.

The power of emotion

Several years ago I saw a shirt that I liked, in a shop in Royal William Yard in Plymouth. I was pushed for time, so made a note to pop in the following week.

A week passed and I was back in the yard, excited at the thought of buying the shirt with time to shop. Sadly, the shirt and several others didn't fit, and I was left frustrated with an unfulfilled desire to buy.

The shop assistant commented on my satchel, which was in fact my mother's music case that I had borrowed. I mentioned that I wanted a leather satchel of my own and, without saying a word, she reappeared with a beautiful satchel. It was a lot more expensive than the original shirt, but I fell in love with it on the spot.

The moral of the story? Buying is an emotional experience. That satchel gives me endless pleasure and is one of my most prized possessions. The assistant didn't sell it to me – she gave me the opportunity to buy it.

How is this relevant to networking?

For someone or a group of people to buy from you, they need to process the following:

→ Do they perceive you or your organisation as great, or preferably an expert in your field? (Why would they buy average – would you?)

→ Do they perceive that you have integrity? Gerald Ratner found it impossible to persuade people to buy, after his infamous comment that one of his

products was 'total crap' (Ratner 1991).
➡ Most importantly, do they like you?

Assess your likeability

I know many people and organisations that are extremely good at what they do and have integrity, but I won't buy or engage with them because I don't like them for various reasons. Equally there are people who will not want to engage with me for the same reason.

To understand more about this area, read the books by Tim Sanders (*The Likeability Factor* and *Love is the Killer App*). According to Sanders (2003, 2005), your likeability is based on four critical elements of your personality:

➡ Friendliness – ability to communicate liking and openness to others
➡ Relevance – capacity to connect with others' interests, wants and needs
➡ Empathy – ability to recognise, acknowledge and experience other people's feelings
➡ Realness – the integrity that stands behind your likeability and guarantees its authenticity.

Networking allows you to demonstrate your likeability and find people and/or organisations that, in turn, you like. It is this quest for a connection that leads to relationships from which business opportunities arise.

Identify your ideal customer

A great place to start is to ask yourself who your ideal client or customer is and what they look like. Points to consider:

➡ Can they afford you?
➡ Will they be pleasant to work with?
➡ Will the work be rewarding or routine?

Identify organisations or individuals that you would like to work with, sometimes referred to as a 'pipeline' or prospect list. In my early days of sales, I was expected to have an ongoing prospect list, which was discussed in meetings, and progress measured. It helps to be realistic but aim to build a list with a view to working on different parts of it at different times.

The value of lists

When I set up The Samphire Club, I had a list of organisations and individuals that I wanted to have as members. Did I get them all? Of course not, but it helped to focus my activity and effort.

These days I have various lists (by area and/or sector) of organisations and individuals that I would like to have in the club. Some I have met, while others are still to be bumped into!

When I sit down with people and their list of prospects, I always ask the following question: 'Are you on their radar?' By that I mean, do they know you or your organisation, have they heard of you – and more importantly, have you met them?

How to connect

How can you use the power of your network or activity to get onto their radar? Start with your network: who do you know who has a relationship with them? I always start with the professional service providers: who do they bank with, who are their lawyers and accountants?

If you have someone who has a relationship with them, ask if they can introduce you (this draws down from your bank of social capital). It can be via email or face-to-face at an event, if all the relevant parties are present. Find out which events they attend, and aim to 'bump into' them.

Another vital area is the online world: social media. Aim to connect with members on your list on LinkedIn, and follow them on Twitter and Instagram. Each platform requires a different approach, and like relationship-building in the real world, this is a long-term strategy – so don't expect immediate results. Share their content, and engage frequently (see Chapter 5 for more on this).

Another thing to consider is which events to attend (which we looked at in Chapter 3). This should be influenced by whom you are hoping to spend time with or meet. It is also vital to measure the success of the events you attend (more on this in Chapter 8). As mentioned previously, too many people fall into a comfortable routine, attending the same events with the same people, then wonder why networking isn't working for them.

Pay attention to existing customers and clients

While networking is certainly about making new connections, it's key to consider who is already in your network, and to value them. After your people, your customers are the most important asset that your company has. This is something I learned early in my career, when I was the major accounts manager at a major logistics company. There have been many occasions in my career when I have pointed out to senior management, to put it bluntly, that without customers, you don't have a business – however good your product or service.

Sadly, it's still a fact that many organisations and individuals fail to recognise the importance and value of their customers. As we identified previously, their emphasis is still on new business and client acquisition, which is both expensive and time-consuming. In most cases, engagement with clients takes place when they complain, or when their agreement or pricing is due for review.

Handling referrals

Referrals are the holy grail, as is word-of-mouth recommendation. Most organisations would like more referrals, but don't know how to leverage their relationships with their clients to get them. Because the emphasis is on client acquisition and hitting sales targets, they neglect to spend enough time with their existing clients. Ironically, these are the people that they have a relationship with, and ideally trust and like them.

A question I like to ask organisations is: 'How well do you know your clients?' The answer is always that they know them well. I then ask them to think of their top three clients, and suggest the following: they should be able to name who they bank with, their accountants and lawyers, the board of directors and, if appropriate, something of their personal situation (partner, family and so on). Very rarely do they know this, yet it's the foundation on which their relationship is built.

The solution is very simple. Invest a lot more time and effort in your major clients. Get to know them deeply, with the aim of moving your relationship with them from supplier to strategic partner. Do this, and referrals will flow – which leads to the next dilemma.

How do you thank them for referrals? Ideally in a way that is personal and relevant (for example, if you know they like rugby, match-day entertainment is your answer).

The value of structure

I sit down annually with my members and agree a plan for the year ahead. This includes what they want to gain from their association with the club. We also agree how this will be measured, and how often we are going to meet to review said plan.

The benefit of this is that it provides structure, and helps me to provide the best member experience for them.

Focus on a specific sector

To make your networking activity more strategic, you could decide to concentrate on a specific sector. By doing this over time, you will become perceived as an expert, which makes you more attractive to potential customers. By attending sector-specific events you become a familiar face, and have the opportunity to build strategic relationships within that sector. (The sectors that I operate in are food and drink, professional services and hospitality. Over the years I have built relationships in these sectors through consistent effort. I keep abreast of sector trends, read relevant publications, show up at sector events on a regular basis and sponsor tourism awards.)

This strategy involves research to begin with and, like all networking, a plan that is measurable and reviewed regularly. This approach is an effective use of your budget and time, and likely to lead to results more quickly.

Work out how wide to cast your net

This is a fundamental consideration when formulating your networking plan. Time and budget play their part but equally, attitude is key:

➡ Are you prepared to travel, and how far?

➡ What type of events are you going to attend?
➡ What time of day?

Some companies I work with cover more ground by sharing their networking activity, and this is something I highly recommend. A lot of companies and individuals concentrate on their local market or a specific sector, as previously discussed – but after a while it becomes more difficult to make new connections.

Additionally, the connections you make will have networks that are similar to your own. It's so easy to fall into a comfortable routine, but this can prove less effective over time. It's important to vary your networking activity and be prepared to venture further afield. (I am constantly looking for new networking opportunities, and relish making new connections who are far removed from my existing network. Because these connections don't know my existing network, they open a whole new world to me – which is incredibly valuable.)

Think about budget

Networking is an integral part of your sales and marketing activity: it needs to be paid for from your sales or marketing budget – so overhaul your budget to allocate sufficient resources to support your networking activity.

Measure your networking

How you choose to measure the success of your networking activity is key. The majority of business owners and finance directors are obsessed with ROI, but with networking there is little initial ROI, which makes them reluctant to allocate sufficient resource.

Over time, it's entirely possible to show ROI – and at this point, to stress the lifetime value of a client. The hard part is to convince them to hold their nerve and wait for the results that will eventually come. In the short term, better measurements include return on relationships and return on engagement.

For every client, try logging the referrals and value of the business you receive as a result. Normally, this will be far greater than the spend involved getting them on board in the first place. Another consideration is how much they contribute to your social capital.

Adapt your mindset

It's difficult to implement a strategy successfully without the right attitude. First, it's essential to recognise that it takes time and effort to build an effective network – it's not a sprint. You have to be prepared to invest time and money in building a bank of social capital, and this involves building and maintaining relationships.

Key traits for networking

Great networkers have certain traits, as pointed out by Heather Townsend (2011) in *The Financial Times Guide to Business Networking*. She advises being selfless and generous, both with your time and your ability to help. My instinctive thought when I meet somebody new is: 'Who and what do I know that will be helpful for them?' Whether I choose to act will be governed by my gut feeling and whether we make a connection. Unless my gut screams otherwise, my instinct is to help. Do I get taken advantage of? Sometimes – but never twice by the same person.

Give freely

The idea of 'giver's gain' is a valuable principle to adopt. It requires you to give freely without any expectation of anything in return. I like to think of it as karma, and believe that good things happen to good people. This is closely linked to the law of reciprocity (people are more likely to reciprocate if you do something positive for them first), which was identified by Robert Cialdini in his book *Influence: The Psychology of Persuasion*. Equally crucial is willingness to accept others' generosity, and to be prepared to ask for it. One of the most powerful phrases is: 'I really need your help.'

Recognise need

A network functions because there is a recognition of mutual need: there is an understanding that investing time and effort in building relationships with the right people will pay dividends. Highly successful people understand this dynamic, and use their networks.

In the Industrial Age, competitive advantage was gained by processes and machines; in today's world, information (data) is the currency that matters: being a well-connected source of information is extremely valuable.

Be positive

Another key trait that great networkers display is their optimism and positivity, which is strangely infectious. Remember the power of former US President Barack Obama's message: 'Yes we can!'

Two people in my network are shining examples of this: one a hospitality guru and the other a business coach. Both are relentlessly optimistic and a joy to spend time with; both have helped me enormously.

Enthusiasm and positivity are great at helping you build your social capital. A sense of fun is also important, as it's all too common to see people taking business and themselves far too seriously. I strongly believe that we all need more fun in our lives. Alongside this, great networkers tend to be kind, and their offers of help come naturally. They are thoughtful and incredibly discreet (think about the information that passes through them!).

Be curious

Great networkers tend to be curious by nature: they're interested in people foremost rather than their business. Think about the questions you ask when you meet someone for the first time; I sigh inwardly when I'm asked what I do straight away. The cardinal sin is to launch into a sales pitch: instead, take the opportunity to find out about them and their life. At The Samphire Club events, pitching is actively discouraged and the elevator pitch is banned completely! At smaller gatherings I get people to introduce themselves briefly, and at the first hint of a pitch, shut them down and move on.

Be courageous

Great networkers are brave and prepared to take themselves out of their comfort zone. They seek out new networking opportunities and are often the first with a question, as well as the first to appear in front of you with an outstretched hand and a smile – especially if you are looking lost.

They volunteer to speak at events and have almost certainly worked on this part of their repertoire. They have a win–win mentality based on an understanding that there is more than enough work to go round, and that collaboration can be incredibly powerful and effective.

My modus operandi

I network throughout the south-west, and have a full calendar of events, but I also go to other networking events and am always looking for new opportunities. Some are referred to me, while others I find by research, but the system is fluid.

This means I'm constantly meeting new people (potential members), but also doing the grunt work for my membership, and can signpost quality events to them.

Be real

A final trait to mention is that great networkers are authentic: consistently true to their values and beliefs.

Set goals

Great networkers have clear goals and a plan in place that they execute. They show up consistently.

Reviewing and forward planning

Between Christmas and New Year, I take time to set my goals for the following year and plan my diary. I review the year ending, evaluating what worked and what didn't, what needs tweaking or abandoning. Where do I want to take the club, and what can I do to improve the membership offering to provide value?

My diary planning involves scheduling the calendar of events for the year (spread across the region) and regular breaks to take time out and recharge my batteries. My personal goals are also woven into the fabric of my year ahead. Something I have learned is the need to keep some slack in the diary so that when opportunities arise, I can take advantage of them.

Try auditing your client or customer base at the start of the year: discuss each individually, and have three piles on the table (keep, discuss, remove). Look at each one and consider some or all of the following:

- ➡ Are they profitable?
- ➡ Do they pay on time?
- ➡ Are they nice to work with?
- ➡ Do they refer business to you?

When I mention this process to people, sometimes I'm told that it isn't done to sack clients – something with which I strongly disagree. There is no point in working with a client costing you money or with whom your values are not aligned: it damages your business and even your health.

Letting go of a client doesn't have to be confrontational. It can be done with tact and understanding, but this depends on the state of your mutual relationship. With difficult clients you can take the approach of increasing their prices to a level where the pain becomes bearable, but it is better to part company.

Be brave, and concentrate on working with the right clients.

Time management

Building an effective network takes a great deal of time; it's an ongoing process – so time management is key and an integral part of your strategy. Organisations and individuals can take an ad hoc approach to networking, attempting to shoehorn it into their busy schedules. Alternatively, people wait until they are between jobs before they network furiously. The problem here is that it's a case of too little, too late: it puts you in a position of weakness, with the danger of appearing desperate. It's OK to change your LinkedIn profile to read 'seeking new opportunities', but you don't want it to remain that way for too long. Your network and the activity you invest in it is your safety net for times such as this.

To network successfully, you need to be prepared to put in the necessary time and build it into your schedule. Discipline is required, as there will be cold, dark mornings when you don't want to get out of bed for a breakfast event. (For what it's worth, in my experience it's normally the events I have to drag myself to where something extraordinary happens!)

How much networking activity you do will depend on variables such as workload and personal commitments. In a team environment, it makes sense to share the load – this allows you to cover more ground and the appropriate events in case of a clash. For individuals, being strategic and prioritising the events that are likely to reap the most reward are key.

Try at least two events a week and some online engagement daily (on LinkedIn, Instagram or your platform of choice). The more time and effort you invest, the more benefit you will receive. People tell me that they're too busy to network, but this simply isn't the case: there is always ten minutes in a day to engage online.

The initial year is the hardest and consists of endless grunt work: you have to get out and about and show up. Building relationships takes time and commitment. There does come a time when you reach a tipping point, become a familiar face and start to enjoy it.

If there is a shortcut to this process, I haven't discovered it. The Samphire Club evolved from my network which had been built up over eight years!

Build connections

The influencers

A group of people that you need to incorporate into your network are influencers and super connectors. They have the capacity to help grow your network enormously, as they have access to some of the best events (they often host them) and can open doors for you. They can also be huge fun!

Professional influencers can be found in professional services companies (legal, banking, accountants, etc.). They are trusted advisors to their own client base, which makes them highly influential. Concentrate on building relationships with them both as organisations and the people within them, who move between companies and firms as their career progresses. Most of them run their own networking events: to attend, it can simply be a case of getting on their mailing list. Another thing to bear in mind is that they normally have a relationship with the business owner and/or the directors.

(A good example is the NatWest Boost events in Exeter, which are always excellent. They have become a priority in my schedule and many of my Exeter members attend too.)

However, be prepared to be patient, as these relationships take time. Professional advisors tend to be cautious: they're acutely aware that their reputation is on the line when they make a referral. Be respectful at all times, and always say 'Thank you!'.

The gatekeepers

Another important group of people are the personal assistants who act as gatekeepers and organise the diaries of the people you want to get in front of. In his book *Never Eat Alone* (2014), Keith Ferrazzi devotes a chapter to the importance of these people: they wield enormous power. The key thing to know is never, under any circumstances, get on the wrong side of them!

Ferrazzi advises treating them as an ally rather than an adversary, and I have always found this to be the case. Always treat them with respect and courtesy and as before, thank them (a handwritten note perhaps).

Getting through the door

Many years ago in London, I was struggling to get an appointment with a decision maker, as I could not get past the gatekeeper (she had a reputation within our industry as being formidable).

As a last resort, I had a box delivered to her, inside of which was a coconut with a card containing the message: 'I give up, you're a tough nut to crack!'

It worked, and I got my meeting.

It is worth finding out if there is a PA network: if so, try and build a relationship with them. (This is the case in Exeter, where the South-West VA Network is active, and has become an important part of my network.)

The acquaintances

Lastly, let's look at those people who appear to know everybody. Earlier in this book I referred to the notion of 'Six Degrees of Separation'. The reason it works is because some of the degrees (people) know many more people than the rest of us.

In his bestselling book *The Tipping Point* (2002), Malcolm Gladwell references a 1973 study by sociologist

Mark Granovetter entitled 'Getting a Job', which has become a seminal work in its field. In the study, 56 per cent of those surveyed found their current job through a personal connection. More interesting is that of this group, only 17 per cent saw their personal contact often, and 55 per cent saw their contact only occasionally, while 28 per cent barely met their contact at all.

As a result of the study, Granovetter (1973) coined the phrase 'the strength of weak ties' by showing that when it comes to finding out about new ideas, 'weak ties' are generally more important than those considered strong. Why? Your close contacts inhabit your world, and consequently are exposed to the same information as you; while your weak ties inhabit a different world to you and your close friends, consequently having access to knowledge and information that is unavailable to those in your world.

As Gladwell wrote: 'Acquaintances, in short, represent a source of social power, and the more acquaintances you have, the more powerful you are.'

Super connectors

Given the time required to build a network based on meaningful relationships, how are you going to find the time to maintain a network of acquaintances? You don't necessarily have to because there is a tribe of people whom Keith Ferrazzi identifies as 'super connectors'. These people (and I fall into this group) not only know a huge number of people but, importantly, are tapped into many different worlds, providing them with an endless supply of information.

If you connect with a super connector, you are probably only two degrees from the host of people we know. Super connectors exist everywhere, but are more prevalent in certain professions as Ferrazzi points out (and I have always found this to be true).

The hospitality sector

The hospitality sector, for example, is full of super connectors, as it attracts 'people people' who by their very nature are gregarious and committed to providing customer experiences and building relationships.

Hoteliers and restaurateurs are incredibly well connected and hugely valuable to have in your network. This has certainly been true in my case, and the growth of The Samphire Club. I need venues to host my events and because I don't have an office, I use a small group of hotels as my office when I'm in their cities – a fact known by my extended network.

A question I'm often asked is: 'How do you get treated like a regular?' The answer is simple: go regularly, and get to know the staff. Be polite, respectful and always say 'Thank you' (sound familiar?).

I consider myself extremely blessed to have a group of super connectors in this sector who have enriched my life enormously (they know who they are!).

The recruitment industry

Another group are headhunters or recruitment consultants. They are professional matchmakers who connect job candidates and organisations. In the industries in which they specialise, they are a valuable source of contacts and information. I have various recruitment companies and individuals within my network, and make a point of looking to help connect them with candidates and organisations.

The charity sector

A frequently overlooked group of people are fundraisers, who have the unenviable task of persuading people and organisations to part with their money. They are always incredibly well connected and liked. They have the ability to open all sorts of doors for you.

I offer charities a reduced membership package to The Samphire Club, as they do have a budget; however, crucially I allow their fundraisers to attend any club event free of charge. I also work with them by supporting various projects and giving them access to my contacts.

The PR people

Public relations is another sector where super connectors abound. PR people spend their professional life persuading journalists to cover their clients and arranging promotional events. As a result they are incredibly well connected and should be a vital component of your network.

Glamour networking

Many years ago, I had to attend the Cannes Film Festival in a professional capacity. I timed my visit to coincide with one of the major parties that take place during the festival.

How did I get on the guest list? I had cultivated relationships with the film PR executives, most of whom were based in London.

PR people can help you arrange your networking events and gain media coverage. Cultivate and nourish them!

The journalists

Closely linked to PR are journalists, who are also well connected: their coverage can bring huge benefits to you and your organisation. Again, it is a matter of building relationships by feeding them good material and making it accessible for them. Make sure you invite them to your events and buy them lunch from time to time.

A sprinkling of super connectors throughout your network will fast-track your development and could lead to a whole world of possibilities and fun!

Your personal brand

Another integral part of your networking strategy has to be awareness and understanding of your personal brand. Most people I encounter are unaware of this. Let's start with a definition from Tom Peters:

> Regardless of age, regardless of position, regardless of the business we happen to be in, all of us need to understand the importance of branding. We are CEOs of our own companies: Me Inc. To be in business today our most important job is to be head marketeer for the brand called you. (Peters and Waterman 1984)

Creating your personal brand

Your personal brand is made up of various things:

- ➡ your attitudes and beliefs
- ➡ your vision and purpose
- ➡ your skills and knowledge.

People's perception of you will be hugely influenced by how you project your personal brand: this includes what you do, and how you do it. How you present yourself to the world has a huge impact: think about how you dress, accessorise and conduct yourself in a social setting. Consider too your emotional maturity and how you behave under stress.

My personal brand

I'm known as a leading networker: I network throughout the south-west, both virtually and face-to-face. Personally, I'm known for kicking off my shoes whenever possible, and never tying my bow tie at formal functions.

I started wearing shirts with cuff links and a watch when I started networking full-time, because I understood the importance of first impressions.

How you answer the question, 'What do you do?' is important. I have a photographer friend who answers: 'I shoot people and dogs!' There is a man in my network who always wears colourful shirts; it's very much part of his personal brand.

Communicating your brand

Consider how you communicate what you do to the world:

- ➡ What do you say – and how do you sound when you say it?
- ➡ How do you write – are you aware of your tone of voice? (Mine is playful.)
- ➡ How well do you use social media?
- ➡ How much of yourself do you reveal to the world?

Share articles linked to your personal brand, look the part and do what you say you are going to do. Perception drives reality, and image and identity are crucial in today's world – if you want to stand out.

A strong personal brand will do four valuable things for your networking:

- ➡ provide a credible, distinctive and trustworthy identity
- ➡ project a compelling message
- ➡ attract people to you in an increasingly crowded world

➡ establish your value and help promote you in your network and beyond.

Concentrate on how you add value, and emphasise that!

Creating your 'networking toolkit'

Another important part of your personal brand is what I refer to as your 'networking toolkit': a pen, notebook and business cards. These things matter far more than people realise or are prepared to admit.

Always use a quality pen: I'm constantly staggered at the number of law and accountancy firms that give out cheap plastic ones. When you're projecting a professional service and charging the appropriate fees, it sends completely the wrong message!

Business cards need to reflect quality and be memorable. The look and feel are important (some of the memorable cards I have been given have been plastic, and in one instance, wood). Spend as much as you can afford, because this is what you leave with someone – it reflects everything about you.

Ensure the card is easy to read and contains all the relevant information. Always carry business cards with you: I'm amazed at the number of times I meet people who don't have one.

There is a tendency for people in the creative sector to produce cards that are odd shapes, or increasingly, very small. Personally, I find this counterproductive: it's memorable for the wrong reason and irritating – these are the cards I instinctively throw away. When I receive a quality card I compliment the giver, scan and return it, as I appreciate the investment. I then share the card across my social media platforms as an example of a great impression made. Invest in a business card holder so that your cards are in tip-top condition when you hand them out.

When it comes to clothes, again spend as much as you can afford, buy a few quality pieces that will last. If you are not confident, engage a personal stylist to help you. Trends come and go, but the classics are timeless.

Managing your network

To conclude this chapter, let's look at the ways in which you can manage your network, and how you can communicate your brand to it.

Keep records

As your network grows, it becomes more difficult to keep on top of it – so systems become increasingly important. People formerly had a card filing system, but technology has made these redundant. Instead, invest in a customer relationship management (CRM) tool as it will enable you to manage your network effectively. A CRM is a database containing information and, in the case of networking, your connections: it's a valuable tool when used properly, and a worthwhile investment. (I update mine after every engagement with a contact, whether face-to-face, online or via telephone.) However good your memory, it's better to have the information stored, and useful to be able to share that with members of your team. Make sure you include all your existing clients or customers in your CRM – not just new people that you add to your network.

If you don't have the budget to invest in a CRM, start by using the notes facility in the contacts app on your phone. (Before any planned meeting I check the CRM to see when we last met and what we talked about; I also refresh my memory on personal details and so forth.)

Rank your contacts

In the same way that 20 per cent of your clients will provide 80 per cent of your revenue, 20 per cent of your contacts will produce 80 per cent of your results. Identify this group (super connectors will be in there), and rank them first. You will need to devise a system of regular contact with these people, both face-to-face and virtually. There will be a second group of contacts whom you don't need to see so often, and so on.

The value of being organised

I'm an advocate of lists, and have geographical lists of contacts for the cities that I frequent; this enables me to message them in advance of a visit to set up meetings.

I also have lists for different sectors and individual organisations where I have numerous contacts.

Keep in contact

One of the most effective ways of keeping in touch with your network is to use email marketing: send them a newsletter.

The power of a mailing list

When I connect with people, a standard part of my follow-up is an invitation to be added to my mailing list. I put out a weekly email that drops into their inbox at 7pm on a Sunday evening. It's a round-up of club news, what I've been doing and events that are coming up. It's professional, written by my copywriter, but we liaise daily on the content throughout the week.

This is an integral part of my marketing effort and worth every penny. More importantly, it is a way of keeping in touch with my wider community.

A blog is a similar way of achieving the same result, but you have less control over who reads it. Podcasts are increasingly popular (and something that I intend to start in the near future). Again, these are ways of reaching and connecting with your community.

With all of these approaches, content is king – it's worth getting professional help.

Use social media

Social media is another integral way of managing your network (see Chapter 5). I update LinkedIn every morning with a post detailing my movements and who I'm meeting. This demonstrates to my followers the reach and quality of my network and highlights the people whom I tag, who find their profiles being looked at.

Organise events

The last thing to consider is the possibility of organising your own events, as there are significant advantages to be gained. First, you have control of the time and location of the event; second, you can control who attends.

Done well, this can be the most effective way to spend your marketing budget (for more on this, see Chapter 9).

Key takeaways

- ➡ Strategy is essential: have a plan and review it regularly.
- ➡ Incorporate virtual networking into your strategy and monitor it as you would live events.
- ➡ Consider hosting your own events.

Networking tip

Add new events to your networking strategy: this keeps things fresh and takes you out of your comfort zone, which is always a good thing.

5 Networking on social media

Social media is essentially networking in the virtual world; it is about building and maintaining relationships and is as important as networking face-to-face. Social media allows your professional and personal profile exposure to a vast global audience in a way that simply cannot be done in-person. It is also a great leveller, enabling reach to people that are traditionally hard to get in front of in face-to-face networking. (I have relationships with authors and speakers worldwide as a result of social media.)

It has become an important part of the marketing function for most organisations, with migration of advertising spend from traditional platforms to digital.

From a business development perspective, social media allows you to engage with individuals and organisations whose radar you would like to be on and work with, and strengthen the relationships you have with your existing customers. In the recent Covid-19 pandemic, social media became one of the means by which people and organisations were able to maintain their relationships and business development function, due to the lockdown and restrictions placed on face-to-face engagement.

Although there are differences between the various

platforms such as etiquette and style, some fundamentals are common to all of them. As in all networking situations, aim to be polite and helpful, generous with your time and knowledge, and establish your community.

Social media strategy

A minimum for a social media networking strategy is daily activity across all the platforms you use. I'm often asked how many platforms to use or which ones to prioritise. It's better to do one or two well than several badly; your choice will be governed by your need or occupation.

For example, Instagram lends itself to occupations such as design, photography and hospitality. Twitter is more appropriate for journalists and PR professionals. LinkedIn is the minimum requirement, so build from there. I'm not an advocate of outsourcing your social media activity – it should be authentic and spontaneous. Do ensure your profile is complete, and consider getting professional help from a copywriter. A professional headshot is a minimum requirement that too many people ignore.

People can become obsessed with the number of followers they have, rather than the quality of their connections. I'm far more interested in who you know, rather than how many people you know. It's good to have a large, diverse network, but there comes a point where it's impossible to maintain a meaningful relationship with vast numbers.

Social media is changing rapidly: it's worth attending workshops from time to time to keep up to date. There is an ugly side to social media, but with careful consideration and a professional approach, it can be an essential tool in your networking activity.

Let's look at the different platforms and how to use them for networking.

LinkedIn

From a networking point of view, LinkedIn is arguably the most important platform. It is the most formal, so it's important to wear your professional hat whenever you use it. If you only use one platform, LinkedIn is the one to choose for both business development and career enhancement: it's your shop window globally and allows you to be found. It's also one of the first places professional recruiters look when doing their research into candidates.

Professionalise your profile

Ensure your profile is tip-top and that you understand how to use the platform. There are LinkedIn experts who can help you with this, and you need to view their help as a valuable investment.

How I use LinkedIn

When I meet someone new, the first place I go is LinkedIn. I'm interested in their career history, who they know, any connections we have in common and, most importantly, what recommendations they have. I also notice the small details, such as their photo. As in the real world, first impressions count.

Do quality, not quantity

To raise your profile and establish your reputation, you should post content on a regular basis (as mentioned previously, consider having it professionally written). An effective way to stimulate engagement is to ask questions; from a business development viewpoint, this allows you to establish the issues with which people require help.

Build a bank of recommendations from members of your network, and aim for quality – it's better to have fewer from key people, than many from friends and colleagues.

Engage daily

To gain the most benefits from LinkedIn, you need to adopt a strategy (as with all aspects of your networking). You need to be on the platform daily (I drop in on a regular basis throughout the day). Like people's posts and leave comments – you don't need to know them – and perhaps share their post. This engagement is an effective way to initiate a conversation and extend your network. (As part of my daily routine, I actively look for posts from my members, which I like, comment and share because as an influencer it adds value to their membership and it is one way I can help them.)

Triage connection requests

Should you accept invitations to connect from people you don't know? Personally, I'm always cautious – it depends on various things, such as who we know in common. If there is a personal message I'm far more likely to look at it, and when inviting people to connect, I always send a personal message.

Company pages and LinkedIn groups

Organisations can have a LinkedIn page, which is their shop window in exactly the same way as it is for individuals. LinkedIn also allows you to establish groups or join existing groups (communities or tribes) where you can communicate with people with similar interests. LinkedIn is a treasure trove of knowledge, with new material being posted all the time.

LinkedIn Local

A recent innovation has been the emergence of LinkedIn Local, originating in Australia. It is a local face-to-face gathering for people who are interested to learn more about the platform and who are probably connected, but may have never met in real life. Something I like about the concept is the gathering is free of charge.

It also allows you to demonstrate your professional expertise without being overtly sales-like or pushy.

Twitter

If LinkedIn is the adult platform, Twitter is the teenager: far more informal in its culture and etiquette. It's a platform where it's totally OK to show your personality – and because you are limited to 240 characters, punctuation doesn't matter. In fact, Twitter has its own language and abbreviations:

- ➡ Tweetup – a meeting of Twitter people in real life
- ➡ Twibe – a group of Twitter users interested in a particular topic
- ➡ Tweeps/Peeps – people on Twitter.

Form social connections

On Twitter you connect with people on a personal and emotional level: it's like going to a networking event where you know everyone. It's about social dialogue, where you find out about people's interests outside of work. Twitter is all about letting people know who you are so that they get to like and trust you. (Anybody looking at my Twitter feed will get to know that I'm a foodie who likes eating out and cooking.)

My favourite analogy to describe it is like being in the world's largest bar, being surrounded by multiple conversations. You can listen, or you can join in.

Build relationships

People wonder if Twitter is relevant for business, as it can be viewed as a trivial platform and has suffered reputational damage recently with the rise of trolling. Twitter is invaluable, and should be an integral part of your networking strategy; but like all these platforms, it has to be used effectively. Twitter gives you another method of engaging with your customers or clients. I always ask organisations: 'Wouldn't you want to know what your customers are saying about you?'

Twitter is a great way to initiate and build a relationship. As a matter of course, you should be following organisations and individuals that you would like to do business with or influencers who can help you. Twitter should be an integral part of your client management strategy too: be sure to follow all of your clients, as you will gain valuable insight into their world and who is in their network. This allows you to react to issues in real time, and enhance the customer experience you provide. Do follow individuals within an organisation, as well as the company itself.

Raise your profile

Twitter raises your individual profile and your brand. It allows you to share your knowledge and expertise, which is one of the basic functions of networking. Like LinkedIn, Twitter is a treasure trove of talent and information: for example, it's my first point of call if I need to find out something. It is a primary news source (ask any journalist – they will tell you most major stories break on Twitter before anywhere else).

Because of its informality, Twitter is a great leveller: you can reach virtually anybody, wherever they may be in the world or whatever their status. (I reach out to authors if I have enjoyed a book – it's far better to give positive feedback and praise.)

Use it for PR

Used properly, Twitter is also an excellent tool for any public relations you engage in: as mentioned earlier, journalists are active users of the platform. I recommend building relationships with journalists for several reasons, and Twitter is a good way to do this. Interestingly the majority of chefs that I know are avid users of the platform – it's their preferred method of communication.

If I want to complain about something, Twitter is my first port of call as you get a far quicker response than traditional methods – especially in the hospitality and travel sectors.

A train story

Several years ago, I was travelling by train from Cornwall to London with my partner, and the train broke down at Plymouth. We had to get on the next train, which was already busy and seats were potentially hard to find.

My partner was disabled and walked with a stick – so we spoke with the Great Western Railway (GWR) representative, who contacted the relevant train manager to advise them to look out for us and told us to sit in first class, which we did. The manager found us and couldn't have been more helpful.

When we explained that we were likely to be late for our appointment and would have to use the tube in rush hour, she arranged a car to meet us at Paddington to take us across town. I always talk to GWR on their Twitter feed, and this journey was no exception. I made a point of mentioning the train manager by name as an example of outstanding customer experience.

Months later I ran into a senior GWR executive at a networking event and told him this story. He already knew about it, as it had been brought to his attention.

Some things to bear in mind when using the platform:

➡ Like all social media, it is a marathon, not a sprint – it takes time to build a following and bear fruit. You have to show up on a regular basis and focus on building long-term relationships.

➡ Remember that everything you publish is accessible to a huge audience – you are legally responsible for your content. Don't publish anything that you wouldn't want your nearest and dearest to see or as a headline in a newspaper.

➡ A lot of people use automated tweets (scheduled using Hootsuite and other social media tools), which is an effective way of drip-feeding content. I prefer to engage personally, and can always spot content that has been scheduled. Similarly, a lot of organisations outsource their social media, but as mentioned previously, the danger is that engagement may lack authenticity.

➡ Using relevant hashtags is key to interacting with the people you want to reach.

➡ It's easy to be overwhelmed by the sheer quantity of tweets, so you need a strategy and way of eliminating superfluous noise.

➡ Lists are easy to create, allowing you to manage your followers and people that you follow. (For example, I have geographic lists for the areas where I operate: Bristol, Taunton, Exeter, Plymouth, Torquay and Cornwall; lists by sector, and a list for my competition.)

➡ When organising lists, you have the option to

choose private (where only you can see the people on the list) or public (which is accessible to all). Lists allow you to manage your audience. (Before a visit to Bristol, for example, I will spend time engaging with my list to see what they are talking about, and let them know that I'm visiting.)

➡ You also have the option to follow other people's lists. Go to their full profile, then lists. Hit subscribe – it's as easy as that.

➡ It is worth investigating Twitter hours – these are conversations held at a specific time and date, using a hashtag to enable users to contribute and interact. These are common and can be geographical or by sector.

➡ Like any strategy it is essential to measure and tweak accordingly. Try tweeting at different times of day, or with and without images.

To gain a more complete understanding of Twitter, do read *How to Twitter for Business Success* by Nicky Kriel. I found Nicky on Twitter and purchased her book, after which I tweeted her to tell her how much I had enjoyed it and she became a valuable member of my network.

Instagram

Instagram is not as old as the other platforms but it is the fastest growing: as a result, it's an increasingly important element of the social media mix.

Exploit its versatility

Instagram is primarily a platform for sharing images, but with the story element also found on Facebook. The live function allows you to host or join a live event with a global audience.

Follow your prospects and clients

From a business development point of view, you certainly need to follow the organisations and individuals that you wish to work with. It's invaluable research and another opportunity to engage with them. (I found my accountants on this platform when they followed me after I had done a talk for them.)

Similarly, follow your existing clients for the same reasons. It's advisable to have both a company and a private account (unless you personally are the brand).

Show personality, and share

Like Twitter, Instagram allows you to reveal your personality and pastimes, so it's an excellent way of finding people with similar interests.

As with the other platforms, you need a strategy and to be consistent with your posts. Again, like and share other people's content. Instagram is perhaps the most important platform for sectors such as hospitality, travel and fashion, as the benefits are enormous. (I regularly post pictures of past Samphire events: it allows people to see how the club operates and the venues I work with, reminding the people who were present and enhancing their sense of community and belonging. It's a free way of demonstrating The Samphire Club brand.)

Facebook

Facebook is the oldest of the platforms and the most widely used in the world. It is primarily a social networking site, but there is a business aspect to it – another place where you can engage with your clients and prospects.

Most organisations have a company page, and Facebook now accounts for a growing percentage of advertising spend. It is another great research tool, and one of the first places I go when I have met somebody to gain an insight into their personal life. It's also a platform that employers and recruiters look at – so it's essential to lock down your privacy settings.

WhatsApp

WhatsApp is a platform that allows you to send messages, and is similar to SMS texting or Facebook Messenger. A major difference is that the messages are encrypted. Perhaps the main benefit is that you can create groups, which allows you to have conversations with people simultaneously. It becomes another way of creating communities within your overall network (common examples are school parent groups and sports clubs).

The benefits of a networking group are enormous. Something I do regularly is to use the voice note function to leave brief messages for members of my network. It is a simple, efficient way of keeping engaged, and demonstrates that they are appreciated and very much part of my community. It takes no more than five minutes, but has become part of my daily routine.

Key takeaways

- ➡ Social media is networking virtually: it should be part of your overall networking activity.
- ➡ Seek professional help when getting started and to keep up with developments, as the platforms are constantly evolving.
- ➡ Social media allows you to show your human side and has an informality that a lot of face-to-face networking lacks.

Networking tip

When using social media, be aware of your personal brand. Consistency is essential, regardless of which platform you are using. The tone will vary (Twitter and Instagram are less formal than LinkedIn), but it cannot be wildly different. Use the same headshot for each platform, and if your brand has certain colours, the same applies. Authenticity is key!

6 Planning and preparation for attending an event

One of the most popular ways of networking is to attend events, whether small or large: on any given day, a vast number of people will be doing just this, under the impression that they're networking.

Unfortunately, this can be far from the case – and the majority of attendees come away unsure or unaware of what is likely to result from their attendance. Over time their frustration grows as their costs (time and money) mount without any significant ROI. This chapter will show you how to plan strategically to attend an event and gain the maximum benefit. The basic principles in this chapter apply to all events, regardless of size – it's simply a question of scaling up or down.

To gain the maximum benefit of attending a networking event (virtual as well as in real life), you need to put in the time and planning.

Establishing your goals

In Chapter 3 we covered the sorts of events you might choose to attend. Think about whether the event fits in with your overall networking strategy, and whether it's a good use of your budget. If, for example, you operate within a specific sector, you should target their events; it allows you to learn who is who and, more importantly, establish your commitment to their sector. One way to decide is to look at goals you might set for the event.

Goals do not necessarily have to be complicated, they simply need to be SMART: specific, measurable, achievable, relevant and time-specific. For example, you could commit to:

- ➡ talk to one new person
- ➡ meet the speaker
- ➡ meet somebody you have identified from the delegate list.

My approach

Several years ago, I attended a tourism conference in Cornwall with the specific aim of meeting the speaker, the marketing director of GWR. This was a company I wanted to talk to about a specific idea I had. I knew the majority of the people attending and the event was excellent, but my opportunity didn't present itself until the afternoon coffee break.

I made myself grab the opportunity, as it was my goal for the day and I had paid a significant sum of money for my ticket. It would have been easy to duck it, but I was elated afterwards as she became a valuable member of my network.

People tend to think they have to prioritise meeting new people (prospects), whereas I find the reverse is actually true. It is important to meet new people, but 80 per cent of your time should be devoted to your existing contacts who are present. Because networking is about building relationships, events are great opportunities to spend time with your contacts and build the bonds that lead to trust. I aim to walk away from every conversation I have with an existing contact, having learned something new about them.

As stated previously, a goal that isn't always helpful is that of looking for a return on investment on your attendance. This normally originates in the finance department, which tends to measure everything this way – but there is a time and a place. Networking by definition is far too nuanced to be measured by such a crude measure, and part of my mission in life is to re-educate the finance tribe on this matter! Other better measurements will include return on relationships and return on engagement, but these are impossible to enter into a spreadsheet (see Ted Rubin's 2014 *Return on Relationships* for more on this). It is entirely reasonable to meet and start a relationship with an influencer/introducer at an event, which will bear fruit at a future point in time.

The delegate list

This is the key component of good planning and preparation, and it's the item I prioritise above all else when I'm planning to attend an event. Not all event organisers are prepared to issue the list due to General Data Protection Regulation (GDPR) restrictions, but many do publish it ahead of the event for those who have booked.

Request the list

If you cannot find the list, ask the organisers direct. It will give you an indication of the type and quality of the event, and can help you decide whether your attendance is good value and aligns with your goals. You can use it to make the most of your time when you attend.

Identify attendees

I divide the list into two: people whom I'm connected to and already in my network, and those who are not. For the latter, I want to establish if there are people attending who are on my prospect list as potential clients or introducers (see Chapter 4, Define who you want in your network). It is this list that requires the most research, as I want to be well informed before I potentially meet them.

LinkedIn is my first port of call, as it paints a professional picture of my subject. If they are someone I wish to target at the event, they warrant further attention and I put them on a separate list.

I see if there are people we are both connected to with a view to asking for an introduction before the event, so we can arrange to meet. I also look at other social media platforms to get a more rounded picture of them (such as their interests and hobbies).

I also look for people within both lists that I would prefer to avoid for whatever reason, as this allows me to avoid potentially difficult situations or nasty surprises. Equally, there may be people attending with whom there have outstanding issues, such as non-payment of invoices.

Check your CRM

It is equally important to spend time on the list that contains people to whom you are connected. For each one, I check my CRM to establish when we last met and what we talked about. Did I do what I said I was going to do? If this will be the first time I've seen them since their holiday, where did they go? Asking about the location of their holiday specifically rather than enquiring about their holiday generally has far greater impact: it leaves a good and lasting impression. Similarly, ask about other personal matters if they have shared them with you and it is appropriate.

If this sounds like a lot of work, it is – but the time and effort you invest here will reap far greater rewards than if you attend without any preparation and research.

Invite contacts to meet

If I identify specific people attending that I want to meet from either list, I contact them to try and arrange to meet (in a coffee break, before the event or afterwards).

Something else I have found to be effective is to invite a group of contacts to join me for drinks or dinner after the event. It's an opportunity to catch up with a number of people at once, and make some valuable introductions at the same time. This enhances my professional reputation as a super connector and is an effective use of my time.

If it isn't possible to get hold of the list in advance, try to establish who from your network is planning to attend via social media, or by sending the event details to people whom you think would like to attend. This has the additional benefit of demonstrating your networking credentials by sharing your knowledge. (One of the key roles of The Samphire Club is to signpost events to the membership.)

The logistics

When you have ascertained that the event is worth attending, another key part of your preparation and research is logistics: the details of your travel to and from the event, and accommodation (if you plan to stay).

To ensure you perform to the best of your ability, you need to arrive in a relaxed frame of mind, primed and ready to go – experiencing the stress of travel delays or parking problems is the last thing you need. Allow extra time for possible delays, so that you arrive in plenty of time; if you are driving, arrange your parking in advance (prebooking is also cheaper).

Awards ceremonies

Depending on the event and location, I usually arrange to stay the night before or after the event: for example, if there is a breakfast event in a hotel anything further than an hour away, I stay the night before. Not only does this save me an early drive, but it affords me an opportunity to meet some of my contacts for drinks or dinner, especially if they are attending the same event.

Similarly, for evening events more than an hour from home, I normally plan to stay; and for award ceremonies, which tend to be late nights, I always do.

Aim to stay in the hotel that is hosting the event, as there will be serendipitous opportunities to meet other people who are attending. I was approached over breakfast once by a man who recognised me from a conference we had attended. I loved the fact that he had the initiative and courage to introduce himself, and he subsequently became a member of the club.

It's a fact of life that the after-parties at award ceremonies present excellent networking opportunities, but the majority of people don't stay, citing work commitments the following day. If you're unable to stay late, perhaps bring a colleague who can so that you can make the most of the event.

If you have arranged to meet people at the event who are also planning to stay, take the lead and offer to arrange accommodation, and so on. It's another way to demonstrate your value. Finally, schedule in some time the day after the event to consolidate your experience and follow up with individuals you have met (see Chapter 8).

The little details

My modus operandi for award evenings is as follows: I block out the day of the ceremony and the following day, and aim to stay in the hotel that is hosting the ceremony. I arrive late morning and spend the day relaxing (preferably in the pool or spa), with a sleep included. This may sound self-indulgent, but experience has taught me that the night will be long and I need to be in peak condition to gain maximum benefit and enjoyment. (I compare it to an athlete warming up before an event.) Given that I don't operate well on minimal sleep, I never schedule anything the day after an awards evening – it's dedicated to recovery, reflection and follow-up.

I have made numerous valuable connections at these events, often in the bar in the early hours. Similarly, I have strengthened my existing relationships, especially at sector-specific awards (tourism, food and drink).

Something I regularly do is take tables at award ceremonies or charity dinners. Rather than pick up the cost of the entire table, I sell seats to members of my network. I also gift seats where appropriate. It's a win-win, as I reduce my costs and they get to attend a fun evening while also making some valuable connections.

This is a golden opportunity to curate a table of people whom I think will benefit from being introduced. It's important to plan the mix carefully, and to be aware of the nuances of your network.

Your toolkit

As the name indicates, this refers to what you need to take with you to an event, such as phone, charger, business cards, pens and so on. You also need to consider your appearance and wardrobe. As with logistics, these are items you need to sort in advance, as it's the little things which can throw you off your game.

Planning ahead

Many years ago, I had to attend a company conference in New York where I had a speaking slot – it was only when I got to the airport that I realised I had left my suit hanging on the back of my bedroom door!

These days I plan my wardrobe in advance, making sure that suit or black tie are dry-cleaned and ready to go. I decide on shirt-and-tie combinations with shoes, so I don't have to waste time thinking about it on the morning of departure.

For women the issue is more complex: contacts of mine keep a record of which evening dresses they have worn at which event to avoid repetition – trivial to some, but professional to the nth degree!

One of the first things I notice in winter is people's coats and scarves; nothing creates a better first impression than a fabulous, stylish coat worn with aplomb! In terms of appearance, appear well-groomed but not over-manicured, with hair and hands neat and tidy. Jewellery needs to be kept to a minimum, simple and elegant.

In conclusion, a lot is required in terms of preparation when you decide to attend an event to network. Goal-setting and research are essential and require adequate time – as mentioned previously, the more you invest, the better the results. If this process seems daunting or extensive, focus on the benefits it will bring, and the knowledge that you're making the most of your time and investment.

I offer a service to members where I advise and support them with this process: it often includes accompanying them to the event and helping them implement a process to follow up effectively (see Chapter 8).

Key takeaways

➡ Set goals so that you can measure the success of your attendance.
➡ Spend time with the delegate list.
➡ Prepare your toolkit in advance and check it carefully again as you pack and leave.

Networking tip

Consider arranging to attend the event with a contact of yours: it's far less intimidating, and can be very effective.

7 The event

In this chapter we are going to focus on the event itself, and how to leverage it to gain the maximum benefit from your attendance. A networking event is a piece of theatre, and everyone involved is an actor who forms a part of the cast of characters. Through your attendance you are committing to give a performance – although every event will be different, some fundamentals are always involved.

Arrive well
In the previous chapter we looked at the importance of logistics and arriving in good time so that you are relaxed and in the optimum frame of mind to operate effectively.

Prepare yourself
Something I do before I enter an event is to spend five minutes doing yoga breathing (normally in the privacy of my car or hotel room). It is an integral part of my final warm-up and gets me into the zone. Nerves are normal – in fact, you should be concerned if you're not nervous (ask any performer); controlling your breath will help you relax into your nerves.

Sign in confidently

Before you enter the room, there is usually a registration desk where you are expected to collect your name badge and register. This is a key part of your entrance, and again needs to be considered. I see a lot of people approaching the desk with their eyes down, searching for their badge, which they grab, and stumble into the room – missing a golden opportunity to create a lasting impression and gain valuable information.

It's essential to engage with the people staffing the desk; above all else, it's good manners. Make eye contact as you approach, smile and engage them in conversation, as they are important for various reasons. Like check-in staff at the airport, they have the power to enhance your experience considerably, so it's worth making the effort. Also remember that the people who have organised the event want it to be a success, so any compliments will always be welcomed and remembered.

Study the delegate list

If I have identified somebody from the delegate list that I want to meet, I ask the registration team if they can help – simple but effective. If you haven't been able to source a delegate list before the event, usually there is one at the registration desk: if so, take a copy and delay your entrance. Instead, head somewhere private and spend a couple of minutes studying it (a condensed version of preparation in the previous chapter). If there isn't a list, try taking a photograph of the name badges with your phone, which you can refer to at intervals: it's a helpful reference later, when you are reviewing the event as part of your follow-up (which we will look at in the next chapter).

Having gathered your badge and engaged with the

team on the desk it is time to make your entrance. At this point you are in the wings and about to enter the stage. A theatre reference that I always remind myself of at this point is 'eyes and teeth'.

Make a great first impression

First impressions are key. In my experience very few people consider this at all, and I'm always fascinated to watch people's entrances. Stop and study the room before you enter, as most people go in without a thought and find themselves in a situation where they are surrounded by people they may not know, blindly trying to find the tea and coffee, or worse still, coming face-to-face with someone they would rather avoid!

Find a familiar face

Instead, look around the room to ascertain who is where and look for familiar faces. Smile when you make eye contact with people, whether you know them or not (especially if you don't). This appraisal allows you to decide your course of action: where you are headed, or who you are going to approach.

Look relaxed

Be aware that there will be eyes on you as you arrive, so the aim is to look relaxed and confident: walk tall with your shoulders back.

Most people will head straight to the refreshments, and there is nothing wrong with that – in fact, it's an excellent opportunity to initiate a conversation. However, be prepared to take a different course of action. For example, if you see someone you have identified as somebody you want to meet, grab the opportunity and get your drink afterwards. If there are people present whom you know and greet you, acknowledge them immediately and accept the opportunity to be welcomed into the room with both hands – it will ease your nerves.

How to start a conversation

Approach a group

If you don't see anyone you know, you could approach a group of people. It's important to consider body language beforehand. If the group is facing inwards without any apparent gaps, it is a closed group and best avoided. However, if the group is facing out, it is open and can be approached. When going up to a group, smile and make eye contact. An opening line that I use regularly is 'May I join you?', followed by 'I'm John'.

Every situation is unique, so a degree of flexibility and instinct is required.

Approach someone on their own

Another alternative that I like is to approach somebody who is on their own, as I know from experience how lonely it can be and feel it's beholden to the experienced networkers among us to put that experience to good use. As you approach them make eye contact, stick out your hand and say: 'Hi I'm ....'

You could also try: 'I've just arrived and don't seem to know anybody here, are you in the same boat?' If the person is one of your targets and you have done your research, you can open with a thoughtful comment (such as 'I was hoping to meet you, as I really enjoyed your book'). In all my years of networking, nobody has ever turned away. They will almost certainly be nervous too, and appreciate you making the first move. By breaking the ice you will be perceived as confident.

Prompt conversation

To stimulate conversation, ask open questions (how, what, where, why), and listen like you have never listened before. Ask thoughtful questions and show that you are interested; equally, be interesting. Be curious, and build strong emotional links with the people you speak to – give your subject your total attention and maintain eye contact.

A common mistake I witness is people talking while looking over their subject's head to scan the room. Another error is to ask 'What do you do?' too early in the conversation as it gives the impression that you are sizing them up as a potential sales prospect.

It's far better to wait for them to ask you, as it allows you to end your reply with, 'and you?' Topics to avoid are religion and politics, but it is relevant to be across the news. Introduce others into the conversation, and act like a host.

Working on your first impressions

People receive their sensory impressions of others in three ways: visual, auditory and kinaesthetic.

Visual

This is what you look like: how are you dressed, carry yourself and stand – and why it's essential to pay attention to your appearance in the planning phase. Avoid too much jewellery and scent. Wear your name badge on your right lapel, as it will be in the line of sight when you lean in towards someone to shake hands.

Auditory

This is how you sound (try listening to a recording of yourself). Take a deep breath to relax, and speak slowly and clearly. Be aware of the tone of your voice (serious or playful), use words wisely, and avoid slang and jargon. Above all, be natural – if you have an accent, that's fine, but don't fake one.

Kinaesthetic

This is the feeling you create: be aware of your own state, and aim to be cheerful and relaxed. People are attracted to passion and charisma; it's infectious. Be aware of your body language – as mentioned previously, stand tall with your shoulders back. Do be aware and respectful of people's personal space: some are naturally tactile, others less so.

An alpha state is a relaxed state where you are aware of what is happening around you. Use your peripheral vision to see what is happening in the room.

How to work a room

Given that you have invested time and money in attending the event, you need to maximise the opportunities available to you.

The ability to work a room is a skill that all great networkers possess, and it is not difficult to learn. The idea is to connect with several people (your existing contacts and new people) while at the same time ensuring the conversations you have are meaningful. It's far better to come away with two or three good contacts than a plethora of business cards with no meaning.

Monitor your time

As mentioned previously, spend 80 per cent of your time with your existing contacts, and the remaining 20 per cent making new connections. This may seem counter-intuitive, but the art of building a sustainable network is to invest time in forming proper relationships – and spending time with your contacts allows you to do this. I aim to leave any conversation with an existing contact of mine having learned something new about them (business or personal).

Be present

When I'm working the room I tend to ignore the food and drink offering, as it tends to get in the way. I wait until the speaker is about to start before grabbing something, especially at a seated event.

The most important thing to be doing when talking to the people you meet is to listen. It's the small details that give you an indication of what type of person they are.

Have a plan B

Confession: I have attended events when I haven't been on my game for whatever reason, and in this circumstance it's OK to let go and simply enjoy the event as a bystander.

Never force the issue, as networking relies heavily on confidence and it's probably better not to squander an opportunity if you are feeling rotten. There will always be another one.

Exit conversations gracefully

To work the room you have to be able to initiate and maintain a conversation, as we have discussed. Perhaps more importantly, you need to be able to exit a conversation and move around the room. I'm sure many of you have experienced being abandoned as the person you are talking to suddenly sees someone else that they want to talk to with a line such as 'Excuse me, I need to refresh my drink' or 'I need the bathroom'. Far better to leave a conversation with grace and empathy, as it engenders a better impression with the other person.

I prefer to say something like: 'It's been lovely to meet you! I would love to continue this chat at a later date, perhaps over coffee, but we are both here to meet people. Before I go, is there anybody here that I can introduce you to?' If possible, I take them over and introduce them to somebody I know. Another option is to wait until you have been joined by more people to form a group, then make your excuse and move on.

Here, I must stress concentrating on making connections rather than simply collecting business cards. I always look to exchange cards with people, and if it hasn't happened, I work it into my exit: 'Before we part, let's do the card thing.' Always keep an eye on the room and be tuned in to what is happening to maximise your opportunities (and equally to avoid people that you might not want to meet).

Catching someone's attention

If your main target is surrounded by people and time is running out or you have to leave, what can you do? I politely interrupt and say something like, 'I'm sorry to interrupt – I really wanted to meet you, but I have to leave. Can I give you my card and perhaps we can arrange a call?' Be sure to go on and follow up afterwards (we will look at this in the next chapter).

How to exit an event

In the same way as making an entrance can make a difference, there is also an art to leaving an event. Many people rush off as they have to get back to the office or perhaps another meeting. This is an example of poor planning. If you can, aim to stay until the end of the event to make an impression.

A simple but effective tip is to stand by the registration desk where people return their badges when they leave. Everyone will pass you: an excellent way to acknowledge them, and perhaps grab a brief chat. It's a bit like sitting by a waterhole in Africa and letting the prey come to you!

The final and most important thing to do before you leave is to seek out the organisers and thank them personally. Why? First, because it's polite and the right thing to do. Second – and more importantly – very few people do this, so you will stand out and leave a good impression.

Tell them how much you have enjoyed the event and how useful it has been, and if they have helped with introductions, thank them. I frequently offer to write a testimonial, and always give them a shout across my social platforms. This act demonstrates that you understand the true purpose of networking – which is to help other people first.

Key takeaways

- ➡ Pay attention to your entrance, and engage with the registration desk.
- ➡ Enter and exit conversations with consideration and grace.
- ➡ Thank the organisers before leaving.

Networking tip

At many events the tea or coffee is served in cups and saucers, the problem being that it's difficult to juggle and goes cold.

I always take a mug (usually branded), which overcomes these problems and allows me to stand out. If you're nervous – as many of us are! – cradling a mug can be comforting.

8 Following up

The follow-up is the most important part of your attendance at a networking event, be it live or virtual. Yet in my experience, this is the part that most people either fail to do – or do badly. We have looked at the cost in terms of finance and time involved with attending a networking event, so it's essential to make the most of this stage. I appreciate that we are all busy people, but I cannot stress how important it is to follow up promptly and in the correct manner.

When to follow up

How soon after an event should you follow up with the contacts you have made? Leaving it for more than 24 hours isn't good enough: after that, your impact rapidly diminishes. Make sure to block out a period of time to follow up, and make it part of your preparation for the event.

How to follow up

Develop a system or process that works for you, and refine it until it becomes part of your routine. As mentioned previously, I always block out a period of time immediately after an event, regardless of the time of day: for example, when I'm attending an awards ceremony or charity dinner, I will always take time to make notes on the people I have spoken to or met. This is often in the early hours of the morning, but I know that if I don't make notes, I will not remember all the details.

This time needs to be a quiet period of reflection: your aim should be to write down everything that you can remember about the conversations you have had – all details matter.

My follow-up procedure

I use a notepad, and at this initial stage I simply regurgitate the information; archiving it is the next stage in my process. I have two groups: existing contacts and people I have met for the first time.

Existing contacts

For all my existing contacts I add anything of significance into my CRM, then drop them a quick note to say how good it was to see them. If we have discussed arranging a meeting, I offer dates to move things forward.

New people

For the people that I have met for the first time, the process is a little longer. I am likely to have a stack of business cards that need to be processed, so I start by entering the details into my phone before seeking out the individual on social media.

I look to connect on LinkedIn and other platforms such as Twitter and Instagram. I also send a brief email in which I tell them how nice it was to meet them, then offer that if I can help with anything to give me a shout. If I can refer to anything specific we talked about, I do – as it demonstrates that I listened.

If I want to develop the relationship, I suggest a coffee. It is possible to streamline this by cutting and pasting preprepared text, but I don't do this as I prefer each email to have a natural feel and to be individual if possible. I also enter the details into my CRM. At this point, I ask them if I may add them to my mailing list and explain that I send a newsletter email on a regular basis.

Be memorable

Sometimes you may wish to make an impact, especially if you feel the connection could be important in the future. Let's look at an example.

Using your network for good

A few years ago, I attended a tourism conference in Exeter where the headline speaker, Geoff Ramm, author of *Celebrity Service* (2018), was hugely entertaining and very charismatic. I purchased one of his books which were for sale at the event, and approached him at the end when he was talking to the organiser, whom I knew.

Introductions were made, I thanked him for his talk and left to spend the afternoon at the trade show that was taking place next door. The speaker had referenced his love of the Cornish cider, Rattler. He was speaking at a similar event in Cornwall the following day and mentioned the hotel where he was staying. While I was drinking coffee in the exhibition cafe, inspiration struck.

The commercial manager of Healey's Cyder, maker of Rattler, was a pal of mine and the hotel in question was a venue that I work with where the events manager was a good friend. Two phone calls later, half a case of Rattler was dispatched to the hotel for the attention of the events manager. She left the cider in Geoff's room with a card containing a message that I dictated to her to await his arrival.

Coincidentally, the subject of the talk was customer experience, and Geoff is now a valuable member of my network. I was chuffed when he mentioned the story at the talk he gave at another exhibition I attended.

This is a good example of the power of a network, and how you can use it for good.

Thank the organisers

One final thing to do as part of your follow-up is to write a note to the event organisers expressing your thanks, telling them how much you enjoyed the event and how useful it has proven to be.

If you have already thanked them at the event before departure this may seem like overkill, and I certainly don't do it on every occasion. However, you will be memorable for the simple reason that very few people take the time to do this: it's another way to stand out from the crowd.

Key takeaways

➡ Follow-up is the most important part of the process when attending a networking event. To omit it is to negate all the good work and time that you have spent preparing for and attending the event.

➡ Block out time immediately after the event to make notes and gather your thoughts: allow half an hour minimum.

Networking tip

To create maximum impact, send a handwritten note to the event organisers.

9 How to host an event

So far we have looked at the three stages involved in attending an event: planning and preparation, the event itself and follow-up. Hosting an event involves the same three stages. This chapter briefly covers some of the aspects to consider if you wish to hold your own event.

Determining a strategy

If you are to successfully integrate hosting events into your networking activity, your approach has to be strategic. Several questions to consider:

➡ What are you hoping to achieve by hosting an event?
➡ How are you going to measure success?
➡ How much budget are you going to allocate to the event?

You might look at inviting people who can help with your business development, or choose to invite clients as a way of strengthening relationships and saying thank you. You might wish to provide value to your own network by introducing them to others. A combination of all these aims is also possible.

Budget will, of course, depend on your resources. Sponsorship is common for events large and small, so consider this from the outset.

Types of event

There are numerous types of event, ranging from business breakfasts to black tie awards ceremonies. Your choice will be decided by the answers to the strategy questions above.

Business breakfasts

Traditionally, these are popular and an integral part of the networking landscape. They are widely used by membership organisations such as Chambers of Commerce and other business groups as part of their membership offering. They tend to be popular with busy professionals who prefer to get their networking done at the start of the day, before heading to the office.

However, they do potentially pose a problem for professionals with commitments at this time of day, such as a school run. In my experience, hosting a breakfast can be an effective way of promoting your company – and perhaps should be a key part of your business development activity.

Business lunches

These are also popular, and can be very effective when organised properly. However, due to time constraints and the popularity of this format, extra care is required to make yours special. They need to be enticed by something out of the ordinary.

Evening events

These can range from after-work drinks to black-tie awards ceremonies. Awards ceremonies are normally arranged by media companies and linked to specific publications. Membership organisations also like to arrange this type of event: it's key to look at sponsorship opportunities rather than arranging an event along these lines.

One drawback is that evening events can impact on personal time, so it is important to concentrate on quality rather than quantity.

Thought-led events
Conferences, webinars and so on are an effective way of positioning yourself or your company as expert in your field. This is important from a business development viewpoint as people like to buy from organisations or individuals they perceive to be experts. It's also an effective way of attracting a quality audience.

Sporting events
Arranging an event around a sporting event is always welcomed, and an excellent way of spending time with the people of your choice. Golf days are popular and a way of bringing a select group of people together. Other options include horse racing and sailing.

Finally, virtual events are an important part of the networking mix, and well worth considering.

Preparation and planning

Gather your events team
Organising a successful event requires a great deal of planning. Larger organisations usually have specific members of their marketing department whose role it is to arrange events. For small companies or individuals where this is not the case, it is worth considering bringing in professional help, if the budget allows. They will have

existing relationships with venues and suppliers, as well as valuable experience. (When I started out, I used wedding experts from within my network to help organise my events.)

Create a schedule

Be sure to allow sufficient time to plan in advance for various reasons – at least two months – but this will depend on the type of event you are organising. Dates and venues have to be secured, and your audience needs sufficient warning, as they will have busy schedules.

If you're planning to bring in speakers, caterers or entertainment. The more lead-in time you can give them, the better. Quality venues get booked up quickly, so build relationships with venues that you like, and treat them as you would any of your key suppliers.

Nominate a charity

Another thing to consider at the planning stage is a charity aspect, which is something I normally do. A gathering of people is an excellent opportunity to raise some money for charity, and there are different ways to do this:

➡ donate part of the ticket price to charity
➡ run a prize draw or raffle.

Whichever option you decide on, you must let people know in advance. If you have a large and vibrant network, it's too good an opportunity to miss (I stress this is my personal view).

Virtual events

If you are thinking of a virtual event, the first decision is which of the various platforms to use. Ensure that you are comfortable with the technical considerations, and if necessary, bring in outside help. A rehearsal is well worth the time invested.

The business calendars

If you are planning to host events on a regular basis throughout the year, put together a calendar of events. Start doing this in the autumn, ready to publish at the start of the following year.

The business calendar consists of distinct periods, with breaks for things such as school and public or religious holidays. Other factors include the start of the financial year, for example, and the festive season leading at the end of the year. There are also sector-specific factors to be aware of: for example, accountants are swamped in January, which makes it difficult for them to get out and network during this period. During the summer season, hospitality contacts are less likely to take meetings as they are operating flat out.

For many, the first period of the year is January through to Easter, with a half-term break within the period. There is a second period after Easter that runs until July. Things can quieten down in the summer when the schools break up. This is typically holiday season and most people (especially those with children), are away at some point during this period. As a result, business activity slows down (hospitality sector excluded), and decisions tend to be put off until later in the year. I tend not to arrange live events during August, using this period to take a holiday and recharge my batteries.

The last period of the year starts when the kids have gone back to school in September and runs through until the second week of December – at which point the corporate festive season kicks in. There is a half-term in October which needs to be factored in. This is one of the most intensive periods of the year, as people aim to complete projects or deals before the merry-go-round of festive entertainment begins in earnest!

The festive season at the end of the year is a period of intense networking, when the emphasis is on thanking clients and suppliers. There are numerous events and often awards ceremonies to attend, so you need to be organised to secure a date in the calendar.

Choosing a venue and speaker

Your choice of venue will depend on factors such as availability, budget, the type of event you wish to arrange and the impression you want to convey. It might be that you wish to hold the event in-house – whatever you decide, it will require planning.

Other things to consider are parking and travel time. People are prepared to travel if the venue is special or there is a quality speaker: these have an important impact on their value. For the speaker, think whether you wish to educate or entertain. Availability and cost vary enormously and will guide your choice.

Attract people to the event

Just as you need to establish your reason for arranging the event, others have to establish a reason for attending. Entice them with the prospect of a valuable, memorable experience, and make booking as easy as possible. It could be an invitation-only event, with individual invitations emailed out. You could also ask people to book via your website or through a platform such as Eventbrite.

The importance of the right venues

I work with a portfolio of venues throughout the south-west, and have built relationships with them over many years. I consider them strategic partners rather than suppliers, and the aim is to collaborate to our mutual benefit whenever possible.

I act as a brand ambassador for them, and aim to drive business to them via word-of-mouth and social media.

Refreshments

These are an important part of any networking event, and obviously if the event is constructed around a meal, an integral part of it. Again, budget will have a major impact on your planning. For me, a minimum requirement is tea or coffee with biscuits or pastries. Mugs are always a better option than cups and saucers, as mentioned previously.

For breakfast, lunch or dinner, consider whether to provide table service or a buffet. If you choose a buffet, always provide tables so that your guests can sit down if they so wish. (Personally, I hate standing while trying to eat at a buffet event – it makes networking more difficult.)

Selecting food

When considering food options, you will need to be guided by your chosen venue, which might insist on in-house catering. Alternatively, they might allow you to use an outside caterer, or do it yourself. I would always outsource this aspect, as although it may seem a cost saving, doing the catering yourself will never be as good as the professionals' and the potential cost savings are likely to be lost due to the time and hassle involved – I have experienced many self-catered events, and know this to be true. As mentioned earlier, it is worth investing time in building relationships with good venues and caterers.

An effective format is sharing boards on the table, rather than separate courses: this encourages conversation and engagement, and allows your guests to eat as much or as little as they like without embarrassment. It slows the pace of the event, as people pass food around and nibble at it, rather than everyone settling down to a course at the same time; it also avoids interruption from plates being cleared away between courses.

Venues like this option because it can be prepared in advance, and is often a better margin. I normally provide the following: a charcuterie and cheese board, fish board and vegetarian or vegan option. Good bread, salad and French fries complete the offering, satisfying larger eaters.

For drinks events, you need to consider canapés and finger food. These days, the options are wide and a far cry from the old days of cheese-and-pineapple sticks. Again, be guided by the venue and/or your caterer, and of course your budget. Dietary requirements have to be catered for and it is essential to include vegan options, as well as requesting requirements from people when working with the venue.

Choosing beverages

When it comes to drinks, be sure to provide an interesting choice of soft drinks rather than just fruit juice. There are numerous options, and alcohol-free options are widely available. It is always better to over-cater than run out, so be generous.

The power of generosity

At my lunch events, I normally run a tab and provide welcome drinks with wine on the table. I announce that there is a tab and encourage people to order whatever they want.

In my experience, most people do not take advantage. It's important to me how people feel when they leave one of my events – if that feeling is one of being looked after, that is hugely beneficial to me and my brand.

This is about managing your reputation. To paraphrase the famous saying by Maya Angelou: people will not remember what you said or did, but they will remember how you made them feel.

Successful seating

When it comes to seating, you have to decide whether to do a plan or leave people to choose where and with whom they sit. It depends on the event, and what you want to achieve. For smaller, curated events I do a seating plan, but encourage people to move during the event. For my larger buffet events I don't, and I leave people to make their own choice.

A seating plan requires careful thought and an understanding of the people attending – rather like a wedding, and it can be as fraught. This is a good test of how well you know the people in your network. As I like to remind people: you need to know who gets on with whom in your network, but it is far more important to know whom they don't get on with and why.

Once I was hosting a table at a charity dinner – it was only when my last guest arrived that I learned she actively disliked one of the other guests on my table!

People will always appreciate being sat next to someone they may have expressed an interest in meeting or, better still, someone new that could be a valuable addition to their network. I have seen collaborations result from a judicious table plan. Another option is to release the delegate list, and ask people to tell you who they would like to meet.

The event

Rather like the overall process, this can be broken down into three separate elements: arrival, the event and departure. All require detailed attention, so let's look at them in turn.

Handling arrival

How you greet your guests and handle the arrival process sets the tone for the event. A lot of people may be apprehensive or nervous and, in the case of breakfast events, may be tired and irritable.

A warm welcome and smooth registration process are essential to help put your guests at ease. If you have a registration desk, ensure you staff it with your best people, who have the personality and infectious good nature to provide an uplifting experience. We can all learn a lot from our pals in the hospitality sector (think hotel reception, airline check-in or restaurant front of house).

Have a cloakroom or rail for coats, with a separate stand for umbrellas (there is nothing worse than a pile of coats). If it's raining, station some of your people in the car park with umbrellas to assist guests from their cars who may not have one with them. It's small touches like this that will make your events memorable and demonstrate consideration for your guests.

The attention is in the detail: provide a delegate list (something I always want). If you're providing name badges, make them easy to find and engage every guest in a brief conversation, make eye contact and smile. Encourage your people to ask them if there is anyone they particularly want to meet, and pass this information to one of your hosts stationed near the desk who can take them to make the introduction.

Assisting guests

You will need a sufficient number of your people throughout the room to help facilitate conversations and introductions. Remember that a lot of people find small talk difficult, and some of your guests are likely to be nervous, regardless of their age or experience. It's worth investing in training for your staff, as not only will it improve the quality of your events, but it's also a crucial part of their professional development.

Hand-holding

Something I do for guests who are attending an event of mine for the first time is to allocate them a host in advance. One of my members will make contact and arrange to meet them in advance before accompanying them to the event. This takes away some of the apprehension, and allows the guest to be gently introduced into the event; it also shows consideration.

At seated events, get your people to gently round up guests and guide them either to their table (if using a plan), or a table of their choice. Have at least one of your people at each table to act as host and ensure everyone is looked after. Personally, I like it when people are asked to introduce themselves to the table before they dive into conversation with those seated next to them. This is something the host can manage in a friendly way, with a gentle reminder that elevator pitches are not required, and that name and company suffice.

If it's a drinks event, have enough people to help your guests work the room and make introductions.

Managing speakers

It's common to have a guest speaker, which is something I like. Aim for something informative and/or entertaining, and discourage sales pitches. Sometimes professional companies put on an informative event (e.g. budget review) with excellent content, but can't resist adding the dreaded words: 'Of course, this is something we can help you with...' This is a given and should never be said, as it cheapens the event you have worked so hard to put together.

As mentioned previously, one weakness of membership organisation events is that they feel obliged to give members the chance to pitch their offering. I've lost count of the number of times I've been at a Chamber of Commerce event, enjoying a conversation, then having to stop to sit through a number of overt sales pitches. (I have a photo on my phone of a Chamber lunch I attended where everyone on my table is working on their phones during a company pitch!)

Concluding the event

The end of the event is just as important as the beginning. Ideally it will end on time – this is important because people have busy lives and you don't want to embarrass them if they have to get up and leave early. Just as you need to take pains to welcome your guests, it's equally important to manage their departure.

Your registration desk needs to be staffed, as this is where people will return their badges and look to collect their coats, umbrellas and so on. Be sure to thank your guests individually as they leave, and engage with them just as you did when they arrived. Ask yourself how you want your guests to feel when they leave your event.

This is also a good time to elicit feedback: it's more effective and personal than a form on the table (something I dislike). Ask your guests if they have enjoyed the event and found it useful. You might want to consider giving them goodie bags to take away (I like to see samples, merchandise or company information in these).

Follow-up

The final part of the process is the follow-up: this is perhaps the most important part of the process, and needs to be done within 24 hours for maximum impact.

Email everybody who attended, and thank them for coming along. This is also an excellent time to ask for feedback and suggestions on venue, speaker, content, food and drink, and so on, which you can use to improve your offering in future.

Also, ask if you can add them to your mailing list, so you can stay in touch about future events. It is good practice to announce your next event with details, and encourage people to book. If you had a speaker, be sure to thank them too. The venue needs to be thanked, again partly because it's good manners but equally because this is how you build a good working relationship with them.

Key takeaways

- ➡ Work out your strategy. Why do you want to host an event, and what do you want to achieve?
- ➡ Planning and preparation are key – seek professional help.
- ➡ Follow-up and feedback help you to work out what went well and help with future planning.

Networking tip

Focus your attention and efforts on customer experience. How do you want your guests to feel when they leave your event, and what do you want them to say about it?

10 The changing face of networking

In this chapter we are going to look at the impact of the Covid-19 pandemic, and how it has changed the networking landscape overnight in ways that will continue to affect networking into the future.

From in-person to virtual

Pre-pandemic, I was operating a monthly schedule that included lunches in Bristol, Exeter, Plymouth and Cornwall. I had also introduced events into Taunton and Torquay. The news of a virus on the other side of the world didn't seem threatening at first, but the storm clouds started gathering in February 2020. The last event I attended was the Exeter Living Awards, a black-tie gathering for more than 300 people, and I do recall a sense of unease. Lockdown arrived suddenly, and my world of live networking came to a shuddering halt overnight!

After a call with my team, we concluded that networking would have to move online – not an area of strength for me. Having refinanced the company, I was in the fortunate position of being confident we could ride out the storm. One option was to shut down, but we quickly abandoned this idea as now more than ever, with opportunities

FOR THE LOVE OF NETWORKING

reduced, the club membership needed my support. We decided to wait a week or so to see what other people were doing, and take time out to make a plan.

Suddenly the world was awash with online networking events, and it was a learning curve for all concerned. Webinars and seminars were everywhere (with professional service companies leading the way), and networking on Zoom became the norm.

My love/hate relationship with IT

Confession: until lockdown, I had never heard of platforms such as Zoom or Microsoft Teams, and had used Skype to call friends around the world. It soon became apparent that I needed to get up to speed.

Another confession: I do not have a computer or a laptop – I run my business off a smartphone and tablet. This is a source of huge amusement among my techie contacts. I quickly learned that hosting a Zoom call on a tablet has limitations: for example, you can't create breakout rooms. Another platform that emerged was Hoppin: again, this proved to be difficult to use without a laptop.

Forming new strategies

Like networking in the old world, strategy was key – it was important to be networking with the right people and attending the most valuable events.

My strategy was to stay visible and make myself available to my membership. I produced a weekly video message that went out across my platforms, and had time to speak with my members on an individual basis without having to travel.

I took the decision early on to cancel all membership renewals and revisit the subject in January 2021, something with which my finance director wasn't wholly comfortable. For me, it was a very easy decision: we could afford to do it, and it was the right thing to do. It was based on membership experience, and factoring into the equation how we wanted to be judged and remembered. As I said at the time: we're all facing the same storm, but are certainly not all in the same boat.

The period in summer 2020 when restrictions were eased a little, provided some light relief – it was joyous to be able to see people again. (I recall a fabulous day in Bristol, eating and drinking with some of my contacts and staying in a nice hotel.)

When it became apparent that we were going into a third lockdown on Boxing Day 2020, I decided to provide some structure for our members, and introduced two regular Zoom calls to bookend the week. They are drop-in calls where members catch up: we use breakout rooms to facilitate mixing and conversation. As with my live events, there is no selling or elevator pitches. Guests are welcomed and made to feel comfortable.

Something else I introduced was a club WhatsApp group where members could engage with each other 24/7, which proved to be very popular. It encouraged relationship-building without me having to be present in the moment. It also accelerated the sense of community within the club, regardless of geography.

The benefits of virtual networking

Networking in this way on platforms such as Zoom has been a game changer and transformed my business. The obvious advantage is the time saved and convenience. More pertinently, it overcomes the issue of location.

How moving to virtual networking transformed my business

Before the pandemic, my membership tended to operate in silos throughout the region: for example, the Bristol members were unlikely to meet or engage with the Cornwall members on a regular basis. Online networking has overcome this issue and accelerated the relationship-building process so that when they do meet face-to-face, the hard work has already been done.

The Samphire Club community has become one large family, rather than separate groups of members based on geography. It has been heart-warming to witness collaborations between members springing up all over the place, regardless of location.

In a wider sense, virtual networking has enabled people to attend events, even in different countries, that they might not have been able to attend otherwise.

The pandemic has also illustrated the benefits of having a vibrant network more than ever before. To have a ready-made support group in place has been incredibly valuable in these difficult times. For people such as myself, it has been a reaffirmation of everything I hold dear, an opportunity to demonstrate the value of what I do and that membership can bring.

By depriving us of the opportunity to network and socialise as we did before, we have had time to re-examine traditional networking models and plan for the future. There is no substitute for live events or getting back out and meeting people face-to-face, but virtual events have been a valuable addition to the world of networking.

Lessons from virtual networking

We have all had to learn the language and etiquette of networking online. 'You're on mute' will be remembered as one of the phrases of lockdown. I love the fact that we get a glimpse into each other's homes, and to see a little of what lies behind the professional persona. (Personally, I like it when children or pets appear as I think it humanises us all.)

Something else we have learned is that networking virtually can be tiring: it has reminded us that too much screen time isn't healthy, and that making time for fresh air and exercise and not scheduling back-to-back Zoom calls all day are essential!

Virtual networking, like working from home, is here to stay; we won't be returning to what went before. What does the future of networking look like? It's likely to be a hybrid of both virtual and face-to-face, with perhaps less international travel.

As the old saying goes: 'adapt or die!'

Key takeaways

➡ Virtual networking overcomes geographical barriers and saves a great deal of time.

➡ It has accelerated the relationship-building process and led to numerous collaborations.

➡ Virtual networking is here to stay and needs to be incorporated into your networking strategy as a hybrid of both virtual and face-to-face.

Networking tip

When attending a networking event online, it's fine to have pets or family members or housemates appearing in the background: it makes you more authentic.

Appendix 1
Networking mistakes, and how to rectify them

Thinking that networking is about sales and selling

This is a common misconception perpetuated by networking groups that focus on sales and referrals. The result is that a lot of people experience networking done badly, which has a negative impact on their view of networking and in some cases prevents them from continuing.

In fact, networking is primarily about relationships (building and maintaining them), and often sales are a by-product of this, along with many other benefits. Focus on building relationships by careful preparation and following a strategy, and more benefits and enjoyment will follow (see Chapters 4 and 6).

Not having a networking plan or strategy

Very few people I meet have a networking plan that is written into their business plan. Most people network in a random fashion: it's something they try to squeeze into their business activity, often reluctantly. This inevitably leads to mixed results, which again leads them to question the validity of networking as a business activity.

This is easily rectified and is something I help people with all the time. It is extremely difficult to network effectively without a plan or strategy, but when these are incorporated, networking becomes easier and much more effective (see Chapter 4).

Networking in the wrong place

Because people network without a plan or strategy, they can end up in the wrong place with the wrong people. As a result, they waste time and money – there is a danger that they'll lose faith with networking in general.

Another danger is falling into a comfortable habit where their networking can become more social than business. This is easily rectified by formulating a plan. For example, if you have identified food and drink as a sector you wish to work with, it makes sense to attend sector-specific networking events. Equally, super connectors can point people in the right direction by signposting relevant events for them. I do this all the time for my members and people in my network, and often accompany them to new events to help with nerves and introductions (see Chapter 3).

Expecting instant results

Many people have unrealistic expectations about what they are going to achieve by networking. This is partly linked to mistakenly viewing networking as a sales function. Equally, there is subtle pressure applied by finance managers and directors who oversee the cost of networking – this can be overcome via education and training.

I spend a lot of time delivering networking training for both individuals and organisations, and the first thing I concentrate on is defining what networking is so that expectations are realistic. Networking is a long-term strategy that delivers huge benefits over time. As a rule of thumb, consider it a period of between 12 and 18 months between meeting somebody and working with them. There will be occasions where there is an instant result, but in general, relationships have to be built before meaningful results occur.

Part of my mission is to re-educate finance directors about networking (see Chapter 4).

Lack of preparation or research and follow-up

As we have seen in the previous chapters, most people do not prepare or research adequately before attending an event; then either forget to follow up, or do so too slowly. It is essential to recognise the value of networking and invest the necessary time and effort (see Chapters 6 and 8)

Inability to work a room

Something I see on a regular basis is people at events who make no effort to work the room. They spend time talking to people they know because it's more comfortable (ironically, professional service people are more guilty than most).

Again, this can be overcome with training and practice. Something I find effective is to attend an event with someone, then separate and work the room independently before reconvening to compare results (see Chapter 7).

Lack of a personal brand

Another issue is that people are unable to answer the question: 'What do you do?' This is asked at every networking event and in most social circles when meeting people for the first time. Answers such as 'I'm a lawyer' or 'I'm in marketing' give very little information, so the questioner is none the wiser and has little to go on to continue the conversation.

A personal brand is important because it lets people know what you do. I spend a great deal of time with people helping them answer this question properly. Consider what it is you do for your customers or clients, and what working with you will feel like for them. For example, in the case of an accountant it's far better to say, 'I help my clients reduce their tax liabilities and help them with the numbers' (see Chapter 4).

Appendix 2
The A–Z of networking

A

Abundance Great networkers have an abundance mentality and are happy to share their knowledge and contacts.

Activity Networking and the creation of a powerful network requires you to put the work in consistently.

Allotment Think of your network as an allotment. If you tend to it on a regular basis, it will provide a harvest for you, year after year.

Attitude Networking requires the right attitude: positivity and optimism help enormously.

Authenticity Great networkers are authentic, one of the attributes that makes them memorable.

Award ceremonies These provide excellent networking opportunities. Be prepared to put the work in on the night; the best networking takes place afterwards in the bar.

B

Brave It takes courage to walk into a room full of strangers and engage someone in conversation.

Breakfast Get into the habit of arranging breakfast meetings.

Business cards They matter, so invest in quality.

C

Charity dinners These provide excellent networking opportunities.

Coffee meeting A go-to option when following up after meeting someone for the first time.

Community A sense that you look to develop within your network.

Connecting Great networkers are attuned to the value of putting people together by making the relevant introductions.

Contacts Your network consists of your contacts, which need to be nurtured.

Conversations Networking is all about engagement, and conversations are a key part of the process.

Customer Relationship Management (CRM) An essential tool to manage your contacts within your network.

Curious Great networkers are genuinely interested in other people.

D

Delegate list Provided at most networking events, a key piece of information.

Determination Great networkers have this in spades, which allows them to keep going when things are challenging.

Discipline Very similar to determination – an essential quality that great networkers possess.

E

Effort Networking takes consistent endeavour.

Enthusiasm Another key trait of all great networkers, this is infectious.

Events Networking events vary enormously, but are a key part of any networking strategy.

Expertise Great networkers are perceived as experts in their field.

F

Follow-up The most important part of the networking process.

Friendly Great networkers are friendly and always looking to help.

Fundraisers Charity fundraisers tend to be super connectors (it's their job to know everyone), and are worth having within your network.

G

Generosity Great networkers are generous and happy to give up their time and expertise.

Givers' Gain A philosophy that all great networkers share: you have to give first to receive.

Golf An important element in the networking mix.

Gracious Another quality that great networkers share.

H

Helpful Great networkers always look to help.

Hospitality A sector that understands networking better than most, and where super connectors abound.

Hotels Provide a great environment in which to network.

I

Impact Great networkers make an impact on the people with whom they come into contact.

J

Journalists Another example of super connectors, they should be within your network.

Journey planning An important factor to consider when planning to attend an event.

K

Kindness A quality that great networkers possess.

Knowledge Great networkers share their knowledge freely.

L

Learning Networking provides great opportunities to learn.

Lifetime value A way of putting a monetary value on a contact (used by finance people).

Likeability An important factor (as put forward by Tim Sanders).

Listening Great networkers listen far more than they speak.

Lunch 'Let's do lunch' – a phrase beloved by networkers.

M

Mailing list An integral part of your networking activity.

Manners They matter – all great networkers say 'Thank you'.

N

Names Great networkers develop a way of remembering names.

Newsletter An effective way of engaging with your network and building your tribe.

O

Open to networking Great networkers are permanently open to networking opportunities.

Organisations Chambers of Commerce and the CBI are specifically set up for networking.

P

PAs Great networkers know how important they are and treat them accordingly; sometimes known as 'gatekeepers'.

Personal brand What you are known for.

PR Another sector that understands networking and where there is an abundance of super connectors.

Q

Quality The better quality of your contacts, the more valuable your network.

Questions Great networkers tend to ask great questions.

R

Reciprocity The currency of all great networkers!

Relationships Networking is fundamentally about building and maintaining relationships.

Research An important part of the preparation process when planning to attend an event.

Restaurants A natural habitat for great networkers; maître d's are super connectors.

S

Serendipity Something that great networkers understand and embrace.

Six Degrees of Separation The theory that we are all connected and can reach anyone through a minimum of six connections.

Social capital The bank of goodwill you have within your network.

Social media Online networking by a different name, and an essential part of your networking activity.

Super connectors People who have vibrant networks and understand the power of networking.

T

Thank you Two words used regularly by all great networkers.

Toolkit It should contain business cards, pen, notepad and name badge.

W

Win-win The outcome that all great networkers seek.

Wingman Also known as a networking buddy.

Working the room An essential networking skill.

X

X factor The secret ingredient that all great networkers possess.

Y

Youth You can both teach and learn from them.

Z

Zoom An online platform to facilitate virtual networking.

Bibliography and further reading

Baker, W. (2007). *Achieving Success Through Social Capital.* Jossey-Bass.

Cialdini, R. (2007). *Influence: The Psychology of Persuasion.* Harper Business.

D'Souza, S. (2008). *Brilliant Networking.* Pearson Business.

Ferrazzi, K. (2014). *Never Eat Alone.* Penguin.

Gladwell, M. (2002). *The Tipping Point.* Abacus.

Granovetter, M. (1973). 'The strength of weak ties.' *American Journal of Sociology* 78(6): 1360–80.

Kriel, N. (2013). *How to Twitter for Business Success.* The Other Publishing Company.

Lopata, A. (2011). *And Death Came Third! The definitive guide to networking.* Ecademy Press.

Milgram, S. (1967). 'The small world problem.' *Psychology Today* 1(1): 60–7.

Peters, T. and Waterman, R. (1984). *In Search of Excellence: Lessons from America's best-run companies.* Harper and Row.

Ramm, G. (2018). *Celebrity Service.* SRA Books.

Ratner, G. (1991). Institute of Directors conference, Royal Albert Hall, 23 April.

Rubin, T. (2014). *Return on Relationships.* THINKaha.

Sanders, T. (2003). *Love is the Killer App.* Currency.

Sanders, T. (2005). *The Likeability Factor.* Harmony.

Schawbel, D. (2009). *Me 2.0: Build a powerful brand to achieve career success.* Piatkus.

Stone, C. (2004). *The Ultimate Guide to Successful Networking.* Vermilion.

Townsend, H. (2011). *The Financial Times Guide to Business Networking.* FT Publishing International.

Vermeiren, J. (2007). *Let's Connect.* Morgan James Publishing.

Watts, D. (2004). *The Science of a Connected Age.* W.W. Norton & Co.